Sociological Theory in Transition

Sociological Theory in Transition

edited by
Mark L. Wardell
*Department of Sociology, Virginia Polytechnic Institute and
State University*

Stephen P. Turner
Department of Sociology, University of South Florida

Boston
ALLEN & UNWIN
London   Sydney

Allen & Unwin, Inc.,
8 Winchester Place, Winchester, Mass. 01890, USA

George Allen & Unwin (Publishers) Ltd,
40 Museum Street, London WC1A 1LU, UK

George Allen & Unwin (Publishers) Ltd,
Park Lane, Hemel Hempstead, Herts HP2 4TE, UK

George Allen & Unwin Australia Pty Ltd,
8 Napier Street, North Sydney, NSW 2060, Australia

First published in 1986

301.01
Sol
141016
Feb. 1987

British Library Cataloguing in Publication Data

Sociological theory in transition.
1. Sociology
I. Wardell, Mark L.   II. Turner, Stephen P.
301'.01   HM24
ISBN 0-04-301205-1
ISBN 0-04-301206-X Pbk

Set in 10 on 11½ point Goudy
by V & M Graphics Ltd, Aylesbury, Bucks
and printed in Great Britain
by Mackays of Chatham

Contents

Acknowledgements

The quotation from the Bernard Papers is included with the permission of
Jessie Bernard and the University of Chicago Library, which we gratefully
acknowledge. We are also pleased to express our appreciation for the
assistance of Shanti Jayanayagam in the preparation of the manuscript;
and to our wives, Hersha Evans-Wardell and Summer Turner.

Notes on the Contributors

Ellsworth R. Fuhrman is Associate Professor of Sociology and Director of the Science Studies Center at Virginia Polytechnic Institute and State University. He has published *The Sociology of Knowledge in America* and has been a Fulbright Scholar at Tampere University, in Finland.

Barry Hindess is Professor of Sociology at the University of Liverpool. He is an editor of the journal *Politics and Power*. His books include *The Decline of Working Class Politics*, *Pre-Capitalist Modes of Production* (with Paul Hirst), *Marx's Capital and Capitalism Today* (with Antony Cutler, Paul Hirst and Athar Hussain), and *Parliamentary Democracy and Socialist Politics*.

Scott Lash is Lecturer in Sociology at the University of Lancaster. He is author of *The Militant Worker, Class and Radicalism in France and America*.

Peter Lassman is appointed at the University of Birmingham. His work has appeared in *Sociology* and *Zeitschrift für Soziologie*. His main interests are in the history of social and political thought, the philosophy of social science, and the work of Max Weber.

Stanford M. Lyman currently holds the Morrow Professorship in Social Science at Florida Atlantic University. He is the author of ten books including *A Sociology of the Absurd*, *The Seven Deadly Sins: Society and Evil, American Sociology: Worldly Rejections of Religion and Their Direction* (with Arthur J. Vidich). His articles have appeared in such journals as the *American Sociological Review*, *Phylon Quarterly*, *The Journal of Ethic Studies*, and *Social Research*. His works have been translated into Japanese, German and French.

John O'Neill is Distinguished Research Professor of Sociology at York University, Toronto, and an Affiliate of the Center for Comparative Literature, University of Toronto. His most recent books are *Essaying Montaigne: A Study of the Renaissance Institution of Writing and Reading, For Marx/Against Althusser* and *Five Bodies: The Human Shape of Modern Society*. He is also a co-editor of *Philosophy of the Social Sciences* and Editor of the International Library of Phenomenology and Moral Sciences.

Derek Phillips is a member of the Sociologisch Instituut, Universiteit van Amsterdam. His major works include *Knowledge For What?*, *Abandoning Method*, and *Toward a Just Social Order*. He has authored numerous articles.

David Rubinstein is Associate Professor at the University of Illinois-Chicago Circle. His article 'The concept of action in the social sciences' won the first annual prize of the Theory Section of the American Sociological Association. He has published *Marx and Wittgenstein: Social Praxis and Social Explanation* and articles in such journals as *The Sociological Review* and *The Journal for the Theory of Social Behavior*.

Alan Sica is Associate Professor of Sociology at the University of Kansas, co-editor of *History of Sociology: An International Review*, Associate Editor of the *American Journal of Sociology*, and co-editor of *Hermeneutics*. During 1984–5 he was Visiting Associate Professor of Sociology at the University of Chicago.

Gideon Sjoberg is Professor of Sociology at the University of Texas-Austin. He is author of the classic *The Preindustrial City* and numerous other books and articles. Among the works he has edited is a collection entitled *Ethics, Politics, and Social Research*.

Nico Stehr is Eric-Voegelin-Professor at the Ludwig-Maximilians-Universität München, West Germany and Professor of Sociology at the University of Alberta, Edmonton. He is one of the founding editors of the *Canadian Journal of Sociology* and has co-edited (with Rene Konig) *Wissenschaftssoziologie: Studien und Materialien* (with David Kettler and Volker Meja), *Karl Mannheim's Structures of Thinking* and (with Volker Meja) *The Sociology of Knowledge Dispute*. With David Kettler and Volker Meja, he is a co-author of *Karl Mannheim* and co-editor of *Karl Mannheim's Conservatism*. He has taught at universities in Europe and the United States.

Stephen P. Turner is Professor of Sociology at the University of South Florida. He has published many articles in major philosophy and sociology journals. His books include *Sociological Explanation as Translation*, published in the Rose Monograph Series, and *Max Weber and the Dispute Over Reason and Value* (with Regis Factor), and *The Search for a Methodology of Social Science*.

John Urry is Professor and Head of the Sociology Department at the University of Lancaster. He is the author or co-author of *Reference Groups and the Theory of Revolution*, *Social Theory as Science*, *The Anatomy of Capitalist Societies*, and *Capital, Labour and the Middle Classes*. He has edited *Social Relations and Spatial Structures* (with Detele Gregory).

Ted R. Vaughan is Professor of Sociology at the University of Missouri-Columbia. He has published articles in major social science journals including *Social Problems* and *Sociological Quarterly* and contributed many chapters to edited volumes. In recent years, he has worked on a project on human rights and sociological theory with Gideon Sjoberg.

Arthur J. Vidich is Professor of Sociology and Anthropology and is Chairman of the Department of Sociology in the Graduate Faculty of the New School for Social Research. He is the author of eleven books including *Reflections on Community Studies* (co-author), *The New American Society*, *Small Town in Mass Society* (co-author), *Political Consequences of Colonial Administration*, *American Sociology: Worldly Rejections of Religion and Their Direction* (with Stanford M. Lyman). He edits (with S. Lyman) *State, Culture and Society*.

Mark L. Wardell is Associate Professor of Sociology at Virginia Polytechnic Institute and State University. His articles appear in various social science journals, such as *Social Science Quarterly*, *Sociological Quarterly*, and *Symbolic Interaction*.

Preface

Derek L. Phillips

In their everyday lives, sociologists often judge various institutional arrangements as good or bad, right or wrong, just or unjust. Further, they discuss, debate, argue and involve themselves in trying to improve the quality of various arrangements. Paradoxically, however, sociology as a discipline is characterized by methodological prohibitions regarding moral commitments and value-judgments. Normative pronouncements by sociologists – in their role as scientists – are to be strenuously avoided. This emphasis on value-neutrality is widely shared among sociologists. Insisting that the dichotomy between the 'is' and the 'ought' must be maintained, they claim that only judgments concerning the regularities of empirical phenomena can be true or false, while those judgments pertaining to the normative sphere cannot be considered in this manner. Sociology must be either analytic or empirical and descriptive, but never moral and prescriptive. In a discipline characterized by value-neutrality, then, sociologists are expected to behave as if they were moral skeptics, uncommitted to any specific moral viewpoint. Thus, they stand mute in regard to questions about the most just or humane social organization of society.

Sociologists not only view normative concerns as out of bounds as concerns their own work, they also reject the very possibility of anyone providing answers to questions of a normative nature. Value-judgments are seen as outside the realm of rational inquiry. There is, from this point of view, no way of offering a rational or 'scientific' justification for particular conceptions of right or wrong, good or bad, just or unjust. Like Pascal, who observed that 'What is truth on one side of the Pyrennes is error on the other', most sociologists believe that normative judgments are not capable of truth or falsity. Thus, questions about the moral standing of a society, or of its political, economic and social institutions, are held to be unanswerable. According to the dominant view in sociology, then, nothing can be said about the justice or injustice of particular patterns of distribution regarding income, housing or health care, or about the legitimacy of one or another political or legal system.

It is probably not surprising that sociologists hold such views about value-judgments and normative theorizing. After all, there was also a long period during which philosophers in the dominant analytic tradition insisted that the normative must be rigidly segregated from the truly philosophical. Ethics, on this reading, was the logical study of the language of morals. The professional philosopher was seen as having no special competence which would allow him or her to make assessments about such things as the justice of a particular institutional arrangement. As was the case in the social sciences, fact and value, description and prescription, were to be strictly separated. Adherence to this rigid dichotomy in philosophy meant, of course, that analytic philosophers were constrained from saying anything at all about concrete moral, social or political issues. Just as in the social sciences, there was a strong commitment to detachment and value-neutrality.

But this earlier agreement between social scientists and analytic philosophers is now a thing of the past. Certainly since the appearance of John Rawls's *A Theory of Justice* in 1971 and Robert Nozick's *Anarchy, State, and Utopia* three years later, there has been an increasing number of publications in normative ethics. Rejecting value-neutrality and the dictates of positivism and cultural relativism, many contemporary moral and political philosophers engage in theorizing that is openly normative in character. Thus, Rawls is concerned with the nature and aims of a just society; while Nozick focuses on questions about the nature of the state, its origins and its legitimate functions and justifications. And Ronald Dworkin's *Taking Rights Seriously* (1977) considers the relationship between morality and the law, asking how morality informs and ought to inform a society's legal system. These theorists formulate and defend principles and standards which enable us to evaluate particular existing (and imagined) laws and institutions from a moral standpoint *independent* of those laws and institutions.

At the same time, Foucault, Poulantzas and the Frankfurt theorists have emphasized how power is grounded in wider networks of sexual, familial, ideological and professional relations. They show the importance of confronting questions about the character, tactics and normative standing of various relationships of power and domination. Gadamer and others in the hermeneutic tradition have introduced what has been termed 'the hermeneutic turn' in social science. More than anyone else, however, it is Jürgen Habermas who has tried to connect explanatory and normative theorizing with the intention of achieving a theoretical understanding which can be used to transform society. I will say more about his views shortly.

The work of these theorists evidences a strong normative commitment to freedom, moral autonomy, self-realization and the like, as well as an explicit concern with providing a rational justification for these ends. Their inquiries focus on issues of equality, rights, obligations, law, authority, domination, justice and the good society. To a large extent, they attempt to provide theories which rationally evaluate the quality of social and political life, that is theories that are 'normative' in the best sense of the word.

In varying ways, these theorists are concerned with providing a vision of a better society: a society that is more just, more legitimate, more authentic for the lives of full-fledged *moral* beings. Thus, Habermas, for example, rejects the idea of value-neutral inquiry, endorsing instead a critical, dialectical hermeneutic approach. Contrary to the view of Weber and others, he holds that moral values and norms *do* admit of rational justification. Rawls, Nozick, Dworkin and many other normative theorists share this standpoint. Among sociologists, by contrast, detachment and value-neutrality continue to reign supreme.

A crucial question, then, is whether it is indeed possible to rationally justify those moral principles that ought – normatively speaking – to underlie and help regulate a society's institutional patterns and arrangements. According to most sociologists, of course, the answer is clearly *no*. Habermas and others mentioned above argue, in opposition, that it *is* indeed possible rationally to defend particular moral principles or values.

In regard to just this issue, Habermas has pointed to the similarity of his own theory of communicative competence and Rawls's theory of justice. Both theories, he notes, attempt to characterize the ideal social conditions for autonomous choice. With Habermas's notion of the 'ideal speech situation', consensus about norms and values is achieved in unrestrained and universal discourse. A rational consensus is that which arises from a speech situation which is totally free from all internal and external conotraints, that is, which is due entirely to the force of the better arguments. The fiction of an 'original position' and the 'veil of ignorance' as utilized by Rawls is *also*, Habermas observes, intended to specify the conditions under which an agreement or consensus will express the common interests of all involved. In other words, both Rawls and Habermas deal with justifiable moral values and principles in terms of the formal conditions for possible consensus.

Despite their common recognition that the justification for particular values and principles depends on the features of the consensus appealed to, Habermas's theory suffers a serious shortcoming not found in Rawls's theory of justice; Habermas accomplishes only one of the two important tasks required of a normative theory.

The first task of any such theory is the meta-ethical one of examining how moral principles and judgments are to be justified; the other is the ethical task of actually showing which principles and judgments are justifiable. With regard to the first task, Rawls stipulates the existence of an original position and the veil of ignorance, while Habermas emphasizes certain conditions under which rational concensus can (ideally) take

place. Those moral principles about which there is publicly acknow-
ledged consensus under the specified conditions are, then, *valid* moral
principles.

It is with respect to the second task – the actual specification of
justifiable principles – that Habermas falls short in comparison with
Rawls. They both share a concern with an *ideal* situation under which
social agreements take place. But Rawls considers this in terms of the
principles of justice which people actually would choose in a hypothetical
original position behind a veil of ignorance (that is, in a situation where
everyone lacks all knowledge of what positions they themselves would
occupy in society), while Habermas focuses on the formal conditions that
would have to be realized in order for any set of moral principles to be
justified.

As a consequence of these differing approaches, Rawls specifies the
particular principles of justice which would characterize a just society.
Habermas, on the other hand, must remain silent in regard to such
principles. This is because we live in an imperfect world where the
conditions defining the ideal speech situation have not been realized.
Consequently, we cannot know what particular principles of justice
would command rational consensus. This is a serious weakness in
Habermas's theory.

Still, Habermas has provided an interesting way of conceptualizing the
relation between rationality and human emancipation. Despite the
availability of his writing, as well as those of others in the tradition of
critical theory, most sociologists today continue to hold that it is sufficient
to explore and describe the values operative in one or another culture,
social system or historical epoch, and that there is no need to pronounce
on the 'rightness' or 'correctness' of these values or of the institutions to
which they give rise.

But in contrast to the situation in the past, we need not accept those
methodological prohibitions that have been imposed upon us and
continue to exercise enormous influence. There have been two important
changes in recent years which help to place the issue of normative
theorizing and value-judgments in a new perspective.

First, the whole epistemological foundation of science has been called
into question by the 'new image' of science represented by scholars as
diverse as Thomas Kuhn, Paul Feyerabend, Stephen Toulmin, Wilfrid
Sellars and Richard Rorty. They reject the view – still dominant in
sociology – that science is an enterprise controlled by logic and empirical
facts, whose purpose is to formulate laws about nature; that scientific
knowledge rests on some things that are absolutely certain; that scientific
progress rests on indubitable truths. In sharp contrast, those advocating
the new image conceive of science as a social activity, with an organized

consensus of scientists determining what is and is not to be warranted as truth or knowledge.

An important consequence of this conception of science is that none of the empirical sciences necessarily has a privileged status in the sense of being able to claim an essential grasp of reality. Of course, in some sciences there are truths (agreements) that are rather well established, that is, which have been generally defended successfully against all comers. As long as nobody provides an interesting alternative which would lead other scientists to question them, such propositions and theories maintain the status of truth. But, ultimately, claims about the correctness of one or another view of reality are always decided in the social context of justification.

A second consequence of the new image of science is that it is an illusion to think that sociology (or even physics) is objective and rational in some way that moral philosophy, literary criticism or aesthetics may not be. More importantly here, explanatory theories have no special objective or rational status vis-à-vis normative theories. All of these disciplines and theories are concerned with justifying their truth and knowledge claims, but none is more privileged in its foundation than any of the rest. *Conversation* is the ultimate context within which knowledge is to be understood.

For anyone who accepts this new image of science in preference to the dominant view (and this itself rests, of course, on an assessment of competing justifications), there will be no methodological prohibitions against making value-judgments and normative pronouncements. But these must be rationally justified.

With rational justification, the status of truth or knowledge is granted (always provisionally) to those propositions and theories which have survived the criticisms and objections of the particular audience to whom they have been directed. In justifying a viewpoint or a theory, the individual tries to gain the adherence of other free beings, employing reasons and arguments that they should find better than those advanced on behalf of competing viewpoints or theories. But even though validity-claims are ultimately grounded in the consensus of the participants through argumentation, these validity-claims may never secure complete agreement.

Hence, as some critics of normative theorizing argue, there will often be serious disagreements regarding the correctness of value-judgments and normative conclusions. But such disagreements are in no way peculiar to the normative realm. After all, the sociological literature exhibits an enormous diversity of explanatory theories. Whether it be Weber's theory concerning the Protestant ethic and the spirit of capitalism, Durkheim's theory of suicide, functionalist theory (of one or another stripe), systems theory, exchange theory, ethnomethodology, or whatever, disagreement is more the rule than the exception. The absence of widespread consensus about the correctness of particular normative theories does not, then, serve to distinguish their status from that of explanatory theories. What this means is that explanatory theories can no longer be defended as having a privileged position in comparison with normative theories. The first reason why normative theorizing must be placed in a new light concerns, then, the consequences of this new image of science.

The second reason is that Rawls, Nozick and Dworkin, among others, have demonstrated the possibility of developing rationally justifiable normative theories. This is an enormously important difference from the situation, say, twenty or twenty-five years ago, and it places the issue of normative theorizing and value-judgments in a new perspective. Let us consider very briefly what has occurred here.

Although most sociologists aspire to the ethically neutral form of inquiry, there have always been others who strongly challenged this dominant position. They emphasize the need to study the relevant problems of the time, the responsibility of the sociologist to offer judgments concerning the value of a phenomenon, and the importance of specifying not only what is the case but what should be so. Many are quite forthright in stating their own value-preferences and commitments, in setting out the domain assumptions which guide their work, and in attacking various social 'injustices' and 'inequalities'. But they generally fail to provide a critical justificatory examination of those moral values or principles which they advocate. Almost without exception, that is, those sociologists opposing the postulate of value-neutrality never themselves attempt to offer a *rational justification* for their value-judgments and normative commitments.

Given the accomplishments of such moral and political philosophers as Rawls, Nozick and Dworkin in recent years, however, we can now see the possibility of formulating systematic theories with an explicit normative content. It has become increasingly apparent, therefore, that evaluative questions about what is morally right or wrong are in principle no less objective or decidable than empirical questions in the social sciences, and that the claims and conclusions of normative theories are not on an inferior epistemological footing as compared with the claims and conclusions of explanatory theorists.

The essays collected together here by Mark Wardell and Stephen Turner serve as clear evidence of a normative turn in sociology. Rejecting the view that there is necessarily a logical gulf between so-called factual or descriptive discourse and normative or evaluative discourse, the various scholars assembled in this excellent volume show a willingness to advance and defend particular normative standpoints and preferences. Rather than simply taking existing social, political and economic arrangements for granted, they submit these arrangements to radical inspection and evaluation. Among other institutional arrangements, they critically examine the shortcomings and accomplishments of sociology and suggest how it might be transformed as a result of normative concerns and commitments.

Like all sociologists, these writers recognize that human beings may compete or co-operate on the basis of a variety of rules, practices and arrangements, for example, as governors and governed, as masters and slaves, as 'haves' and 'have nots' and in countless other ways. But in contrast to the position taken by most other sociologists, they are concerned with the important normative question: which of these specified rules, practices, and arrangements are morally justified, and why? By turning our attention to what is permissible and impermissible, to what we may and may not do, they sensitize us to the need of achieving a theoretical understanding which can be used to help improve and transform society. For such an accomplishment, we must be deeply grateful.

PART I

Introduction:
Dissolution of the Classical Project

Mark L. Wardell and Stephen P. Turner

'What happened to the project typified by Marx, Weber, Durkheim and others of the classical era'?[1] Sociological theory increasingly has become a detached enterprise of abstract problems. Contemporary systems theorists, such as Luhmann, attempt to give general accounts of differentiation, trust, power and the like. Habermas recently attempted to develop a general account of communication. Jeff Alexander has argued, in a defense of Parsonian theorizing but equally apropos other contemporary efforts, that theoretical logic in sociology largely constitutes an autonomous intellectual enterprise because the problems encountered cannot be properly resolved through empirical observations, ideological arguments or methodological considerations. Some recent Marxist theorists, especially Althusser, have pursued a similar abstract theoretical logic.

The abstractions of the classics, though, were part of a project in which understanding the importance of prevailing modes of organization had immediate implications for everyday schemes of moral and political action and belief. Durkheim believed that the emerging liberal society of France required new modes of socialization and proposed particular moral reforms for education. Weber thought that the modern nation-state which was a great power, as Germany had just become, required a new political ethos of responsibility. Marx believed that the emergence of the industrial-capitalist social formation brought with it new forms of exploitation which demanded a new consciousness of kind as well as a new political organization.

Most sociologists today, particularly in the United States, adhere to the claim of a separation between sociological discourse and moral or political concerns. The net result of this adherence has been a waning of the immediacy of sociological theories, coupled with a reluctance to acknowledge the role of moral and political motivations in the act of theorizing itself. Plus, the vast majority of contemporary sociological activity contributes very little to constructing theories having an integrated stance toward whole societies, a major purpose of the classical project. In sum, the key identifying features of the original project are now only dimly visible in sociological theory, indicating a dissolution of theorizing as practiced by the classical sociologists.

In contrast to some recent discussions of the classics (for example, Rhea, 1981), the present volume intends neither to offer new interpretations of classical sociological theories nor to demonstrate their continued usefulness. Our task is to discuss aspects of, and reasons for, the dissolution of the classical project, to explore the possibility of its reconstruction, and to assess the classical project as a model for future theoretical developments which promise an enhanced understanding of the social issues, in addition to their moral and political immediacy, in modern social life.

The Classical Project

The emergence of the classical sociological project coincided with the transformation of Western societies during the nineteenth century. As these societies became organized more in terms of industry and commerce than agriculture, large numbers of people migrated to cities from rural areas, and the nation-state took center stage in political life. People increasingly related to each other in impersonal ways as relationships became predicated on exchange, that is human beings acting toward one another in terms of market principles (Marx, 1976; Polanyi, 1944), and as the rise of mass armies and mass politics followed the Napoleonic model. In various ways, these transformations necessitated new forms of social control and discipline.

The immediacy and thematic coherence of early sociology results from the visible presence of these changes: the founders of the classical project wanted to account for the transformation of the industrial-captialist/nation-state. Their angle of vision was necessarily broad. Politics, economics, religion, morals, the family and the organization of work were the arenas of transformation, and changes in one often conflicted with the organization of another. The 'problem' was to imagine a future in which the contradictions of the present would be resolved.

The task of analysis was in part to contribute to these changes. Saint-Simon and Comte saw the changes accompanying the industrial-capitalist transformation as irreversible, but not nearly complete. The project they sought to establish would 'satisfy our most urgent intellectual necessities, and even the most imperative needs of *immediate* social practice' (Comte, 1975, p. 195; our emphasis), by guiding the transformation as it occurred. Contributing to the intellectual basis for the transformation of society was the focus for this project, with order and progress the appropriate theoretical focuses. An important feature of the project was to reform social discourse, as Comte put it, to establish social thought at a level of comprehension and universal validity similar to the physical sciences, and claim the intellectual authority appropriate to positive science. With Saint-Simon, Comte concluded that the failure of the French Revolution had been an intellectual failure too, which disclosed the limited malleability of the social world. Comte elaborated this conclusion in an argument that outcomes to political action cannot deviate widely from parameters determined by the laws of societal development.

Comte, a teleological rationalist, thus had a progressive vision of the future. He believed that to be rational is to be moral, that the true moral nature of human beings can be realized in the successful institutionalization of positive discourse as the discourse of society, and that political action becomes more rational as citizens come to comprehend the natural laws of society. Order would be attained in the process of change as benevolence for others and reverence for humanity came to be embraced during the course of rational political action. Comte believed that societies develop in the direction of this morality.[2]

Max Weber and Emile Durkheim retained many of the distinctive features of the classical project found in the works of Saint-Simon and Comte, but their audience and aims differed. Where the earlier generation had been obsessively concerned with the extension of sociological discourse throughout society, Weber and Durkheim sought to institutionalize the project as a legitimate academic discipline. For this reason, they attempted to fashion sociological discourse to resemble other scientific discourses of their day. Still, neither Weber nor Durkheim adopted a narrow theoretical angle of vision for the project. Their theorizing continued to cover a broad range of social phenomena with political, economic and religious institutions the focuses of their theoretical works, and their empirical approach remained, for the most part, a comparative method sensitive to history (cf. Durkheim, 1938, pp. 138–9; Weber, 1949).

Weber and Durkheim did not share the naïve teleological rationalism of the earlier generation, yet both admitted that sociological theorizing and theories had a moral/political aspect. Weber (1949) attempted in his methodological writings to assess the impact on theorizing of 'valuations' which influence the selection of the conceptual categories used to construct causal interpretations of historical sequences. He conceded that these selections escape scientific justification. He also openly endorsed the notion that the insights of sociological analysis could guide the political reconstruction of German society following the First World War (Weber, 1978, pp. 1381–469). Similarly, Durkheim did not conceal the political ramifications of his theoretical project. Bellah (1973, pp. x, xxii) notes that Durkheim as a 'philosopher and a moralist ... [was not] satisfied with what is ... [Indeed] a major function of sociology [according to Durkheim] is to provide the basis for effecting social change.' So the project of sociological theory, as outlined by Weber and Durkheim, continued to mediate between what is and what should be, the present and the future, rather than merely reflecting or describing the extant social conditions. The task of mediation, however, was altered by the hands of this succeeding generation of the classical project.

In their preoccupation to gain legitimacy for sociology as a special academic discipline, Weber and Durkheim clung firmly to a notion that the moral/political elements of the project must be separated from scientific discourse. Durkheim (1938, p. xl, footnote 2), claiming to side-step the 'positivist metaphysics of Comte and Spencer', that is, their teleological rationalism, lamented that most social scientists of his day still were too willing 'to set forth in a few pages or phrases the very essence of the most complex phenomena' (1938, p. xlvi) without any reference to the 'things' which comprise the social world. While there had been some progress toward establishing sociology as a unique science, he speculated that acceptance by the full scientific community would not be achieved until the remnants of metaphysical reasoning were rooted from sociological discourse.

Both Durkheim and Weber offered suggestions for bolstering the position of sociology as a science. Durkheim's prescription was the systematic application of a comprehensive set of rules covering each major step in the process of theorizing. Weber (1946) stressed the value-neutrality of sociology as a science; the recognition that the discourse of sociology is not free of presuppositions meant that sociological inquiry could not prescribe the way social life should be, for any prescriptions would ultimately rest on prior valuative commitments.

On several occasions Weber (e.g. 1946, p. 150) unwittingly reveals a parodoxical position which accompanies his notion of separating sociological discourse from political practice. For instance, when he poses the question 'what then does science actually and positively contribute to practical and personal "life"?' Weber answers without hesitation. Science, he says, enables the technical control of life because it provides the formal logic and experience for socializing productive people and promotes clarity of thought when selecting appropriate means for various practical ends. This kind of rational discourse, according to Weber, is in itself amoral and apolitical. But, if widely utilized in everyday practical behavior, it becomes a feature of moral and political life, and its impact will be potentially as great as a change in 'political' values.

In spite of his philosophically motivated adherence to the doctrine of value-freedom, Weber's sociological and theoretical writings often impart an explicit moral and political immediacy. A theoretical term such as 'bureaucracy' for Weber described a tangible present – a class of real persons, bureaucrats, with a particular mentality, who inhabit this social formation and who are in turn formed by it. The political reality that the citizens of Germany acquiesced in the ways of bureaucracy confronted Weber with an immediate problem – both a 'cognitive' problem of understanding bureaucracy as a political factor, and a political problem of constructing allegiances or constitutional forms which countervailed this troublesome reality.

The separation of fact and value which Durkheim and Weber endorsed, each in his own way, was not accepted by the other major contributor to the classical project. Marx (1976) saw the purpose of the project as developing theories of societies which focused on the social relations mediating between various agents in society, rather than on the various institutional arrangements which comprise societies. On one level, he furthered the Saint-Simonian and Comtean aim of understanding the processes by which the social organization of societies was simultaneously maintained and transformed, processes which he analyzed in terms of the contradictory tendencies found in the dialectical nature of social relations and expressed in class societies by the struggles between laborers and owners of the means of production. On another level, Marx wanted to know how different aspects of a society, such as production organizations and religions, contribute to the processual relation between order and change within different historical forms of society, and this was the foundation of his critique of claims for universal ideas. A moral code of benevolence within a class society, for instance, was only an ideology, or a disguise, of the exploitative relations which specified the conditions of struggle.

In contrast to Weber and Durkheim, Marx did not treat the 'scientific community' as holding a privileged status, immune from ideological infiltration. 'Sociological' discourse, as well as scientific discourse generally, are products of people living within the confines of a progressing society, and accordingly 'scientific' concepts of social life cannot be abstracted from the practical surroundings in that society – concepts necessarily carry with them moral and political burdens for their users. Marx (1967) did not attempt to evade these burdens in his own theoretical inquiries. His methodological query purposely combines moral and political value-assumptions with 'sociological' analysis to produce a critical theory of society, and the purpose of theory is to guide praxis (Freiberg, 1979, *passim*).

Marx had no inclination to see either his 'sociological' discourse or his theoretical project become institutionalized within the academy. He saw the academy, just as any major institution within society, contributing more to the reproduction of 'what is' than to the creation of 'what should be', thereby limiting the political impetus of the theoretical project to improve upon the existing social relations. In a sense, Marx's selection of audiences and his deliberate abandonment of academic life represents an intentional effort to escape the contradiction underlying the paradoxes to be confronted later by Weber and Durkheim: how do you develop sociological theories of society, designed with an immediacy to change various institutional arenas in society, while seeking legitimation of your efforts within those arenas?

The Recent Form of the Project

Marx, Durkheim and Weber retained to a large extent the theoretical scope and concerns for abstract as well as practical problems found in the works of Saint-Simon and Comte. Only the aim of abstraction, however, has survived the process of institutionalization which accompanied the following generations of sociologists, where highly differentiated discourses are reproduced along lines of organizational convenience. The 'advantages of the division of labor' of which Weber so casually speaks in 'Science as a vocation' gradually have evolved into a cage of iron.

By the 1940s and 1950s, the classical project was, according to most sociologists, archaic at best; at worst, it was unspecific and loosely formulated. Parsons began during this time to advance the notion that sociology had great, but unrealized, potential as a mature science. In 1945, he wrote somewhat optimistically that sociology

> has not enjoyed the kind of integration and directed activity which only the availability and common acceptance and employment of a well-articulated generalized theoretical system can give to a science. The main framework of such a system is, however, now available, though this fact is not as yet very generally appreciated and much in the way of development and refinement remains to be done on the purely theoretical level, as well as its systematic use and revision in actual research. It may therefore be held that *we stand on the threshold of a definitely new era* in sociology and the neighboring social science fields. (Parsons, 1954 [1945], p. 212; our emphasis)

Merton agreed with Parsons's assessment that the classical project lacked maturity as a science and promoted the new project of developing a 'well-articulated generalized theoretical system'. Merton's (1967, p. 39) recommendation for building this system was to start with theories of the middle range which 'lie between ... working hypotheses ... and the all-inclusive systematic efforts to develop a unified theory that will explain all observed uniformities of social behavior, social organizations, and social change'. Unfortunately, Merton's plea for middle range theories legitimated the development of disparate sociological theories, not the integrated system of higher generalizations he expected. A disarray of new theoretical perspectives emerged which offer little prospect for integration, and a plethora of 'theories of' institutions, processes and dimensions currently exist, adding up to an incoherent view of society. Today, forty years after Parsons (1954 [1945], p. 212) thought 'sociology is just in the process of emerging into the status of a mature science', and almost twenty years after Merton (1967, p. 51) foresaw a 'progressively comprehensive sociological theory which ... gradually consolidates theories of the middle range', there are good reasons for questioning the task, as well as the aspirations, of the Parsons–Merton project. Today issues such as the possibility of nuclear war (compounded by the 'Superpowers' phenomenon) or a world economy tightly integrated around multinational corporations (leaving poverty, military dictatorships and a polluted environment in their wake) beg for understanding. We lack ways of theoretically locating these issues within larger social-historical contexts because they have emerged, in a sense, outside the angle of vision of nearly all contemporary sociological theories.

Sociological theory at present consists largely of reified conceptual debris from the project of Weber, Durkheim and Marx. Gone, for the most part, are the broad theoretical views which were intended as the basis for the development of an integrated stance toward whole societies or relations among societies. Gone is the kind of discourse which moved frequently and fluidly between discussions of moral, political and economic structures. Gone too is the moral and political immediacy of the project, the feature which enabled sociological theory to serve as an historical agent.

The chapters of this book explore the dissolution of the classical project of sociological theory. The essays in Part II describe some of the restrictions which bound sociological discourse. Part III contains discussions of the reification and loss of applicability of certain sociological concepts. Finally, Part IV includes three different suggestions for possible ways of reconstructing the aims of the project.

Notes

1 To say that Marx, Weber and Durkheim were representative of the classical era does not imply that they adopted a similar theoretical stance. Though their theoretical accounts differ, they all were decidedly interested in social organizational accounts of society, as opposed to purely moral, political or economic accounts. In this volume, we do not explicitly engage in discussions of the rightness or wrongness of classical theories; we focus on the contrasts between them and more contemporary efforts.

2 This faith, naïve as it perhaps sounds today, was shared with his contemporaries, such as Mill, Buckle, Spencer and Quetelet, who saw social science as contributing to the fulfillment of humankind through rationalization. This early generation of sociologists

sought the education of the workers – Comte held astronomy classes, Mill donated copies of A *System of Logic* to workingmen's clubs, Quetelet wrote popular statistics books in cheap editions, and Spencer created a series of volumes which served many houses as a kind of encyclopaedia.

PART II

NARROWING OF
SOCIOLOGICAL DISCOURSE

1

Sociological Nemesis: Parsons and Foucault on the Therapeutic Disciplines

John O'Neill

In Memoriam Michel Foucault
1926–1984

The Chronic 'Crisis' of Sociology

Sociologists have cried wolf so often with respect to the crises of society, it will only cause cynical amusement to find the wolf at sociology's own door. Let us suppose sociology is in 'crisis'. After all, how long did sociologists expect to live off the difficulties of modern society without finding that their own practice is as much a part of the society they claim to discover, analyze, administer or reform as the social objects – crime, sexuality, mental illness, alienation, stratification, bureaucracy – which sociologists claim to manipulate?

Only a naïve belief in sociological immunity, purchased through adherence to out-moded canons of scientific distantiation (Wilson, 1977), could have sustained sociologists in the hope that their profession might prosper without crises. Serenely anchored in value-neutrality, removed from and innocent of the war of values, ideologies and conflict which unsettles their society, sociologists have imagined they could live off a troubled land without one day waking to find its sorrows within their own house (O'Neill, 1972). No wonder this sociological slumber is now disturbed by voices arguing that the very practice of sociology belongs to the sickness of the society which it claims to minister. In short, the current 'crisis' of sociology affects *both* patient and physician of the social sciences. Thus it is not a matter of bewailing the failure of sociology to achieve scientific maturity, to entrench itself as a profession, to underwrite itself with government funding, or to be heard on national and international issues (Eisenstadt and Curelarau, 1975). Sociology has succeeded on all these fronts, just like medicine. Indeed, our sociology has achieved a central place in the therapeutic state, alongside medicine, psychoanalysis and econometric forecasting. By the same token, there are signs that the therapeutic state is in crisis because of the very practice of its own strategies for the administration of the body politic (Navarro, 1979). A fancy version of the 'crisis' of sociology is to locate its illness in the brain rather than to locate it in the body politic, as instead we shall argue Cognitive troubles, however painful, are more flattering to the sociological profession and in turn invite its higher specialists – the epistemologist as brain surgeon – to consider the cure to be available only through submission to their brand of rationality. Thus, R. K. Merton (1975) has chided Gouldner (1970) for not seeing that there really never was a time when sociology was not in a 'coming crisis', either because of the troubles of the society which called for sociological intervention, or else because of sociology's own troubled sense of its inability to meet the challenges which might otherwise assure its place in the double hierarchy of science and society. As Merton sees it, the 'crisis' in sociology is *chronic* because of the ever expanding troubles of modern society which multiply its opportunities, creating a *'crisis of prosperity'*, as well as what we would call a *crisis of confidence*, arising from the disparity between the limited knowledge gained by sociologists and the complexity of the practical issues calling for sociological know-how. The 'crisis of confidence', as Merton sees it, is due to the loss of the realist paradigm in the natural sciences. The latter sciences are now known to develop like other social institutions – however they do – while the established social sciences continue to treat their own development according to the canons of an out-moded realist view of science.

Uncertainty and Community in the Social Sciences

What sociology has lost – although the realization is not very widespread – is the same certainty that the natural sciences have had to forgo. For some reason, this discovery about science is attributed to the social sciences. It properly belongs to the work of the medical researcher Ludwick Fleck (1979), who made it clear that the practice of science looks much like that of behavior in other social institutions bound by a collective style or code of activities whose purpose is to facilitate those occasional paradigm breaks which Kuhn (1962) called scientific revolutions. The point, however, is not so much to conclude hastily that if revolutions are the wheel of science then the same should hold for society in general. Rather, what is at stake is the collapse of a realist or correspondence theory of knowledge which once enabled the adherents of science to demarcate what is knowledge 'really' from what is to be considered pseudo-knowledge, namely, such things as sociology (O'Neill, 1983c).

In the particular case of the social sciences, the result of the collapse of the realist view of science is that we cannot so strictly separate common-sense knowledge from sociological knowledge because each mode of knowledge is tied to community or institutional values. What is good sociological knowledge may answer well enough to the values and practices of the community of professional sociologists. What is good common-sense knowledge of social events and processes is equally answerable to local community standards. But whereas nature is indifferent to the rivalry of scientific communities, human beings cannot be indifferent to the rivalry between their common-sense knowledge of themselves and their institutions and the presumed superiority of similar knowledge generated by professional social scientists (O'Neill, 1983b). Moreover, sociological knowledge is not superior – as was once thought – because it is 'value free' whereas common-sense knowledge is hopelessly ethical. Rather, both knowledges are appropriately descriptive and evaluative when and as they need to be; and neither is ever wholly the one or the other.

To suppose that sociological knowledge could ever be wholly descriptive is to imagine a science produced without the practices of the community of scientists as we know them. Similarly, to suppose that sociological knowledge could ever be value free is to imagine a society uninhabited by moral agents like ourselves and steered instead by moral administrators in the name of a system which even natural scientists have not yet discovered. What sociologists have to chasten themselves with is the realization that they are not privy to any higher knowledge, however well formed their knowledge (as in limited ways it is). Sociologists must bow to the inextricability of causal and hermeneutical accounts of human behavior and institutions (O'Neill, 1983a). To suppose otherwise is to deface human institutions and to step outside of the accountability which is a constitutive feature of democratic society (O'Neill, 1979).

The Disciplinary Society: Foucault on Bio-Power

The lesson many social scientists have still to learn about sociological discourse and its dual function as descriptive and prescriptive conduct is forcibly expressed by Rorty in the following remarks.

The idea that only a certain vocabulary is suited to human beings or human societies, that only that vocabulary permits them to be 'understood', is the seventeenth century myth of 'nature's own vocabulary' all over again. If one sees vocabularies as instruments for coping with things rather than as representations of their intrinsic natures, then one will not think that there is an intrinsic connection or an intrinsic lack of connection between 'explanation' and 'understanding' – between being able to predict and control people of a certain sort and being able to sympathise and associate with them, to view them as fellow citizens. (Rorty, 1983, p. 163)

Foucault (1977, 1980a) has heightened our consciousness of the role of social science discourse in the production of what he describes as the disciplinary *society*. This society is the product of historically contingent discourses constructed through concerns with reason, madness, health, disease, punishment, labor, idleness, intelligence and sexuality. These discourses evolved in the shift from medievalism to mercantile and industrial capitalism when the mechanisms of social control had to be redesigned to administer individuals more closely than church, parish and family authority could accomplish. The factory system, urbanism and the new demography of larger populations with endemic problems of labor discipline, forced unemployment, disease, criminality and rebelliousness, made it imperative to recast social control in terms of the humane, reformist and therapeutic model of the social sciences. Because he is anxious to separate himself from Marxist theories of state power and ideology, Foucault translates the problem of social control out of the terms of class conspiracy into the history of the scientization of power/knowledge produced in the double context of population policy and clinical medicine designed to administer the body politic in a twofold discourse.

> In concrete terms, starting in the seventeenth century, this power over life evolved in two basic forms ... One of these poles – the first to be formed, it seems – centered on the *body as a machine*: its disciplining, the optimisation of its capabilities, the extortion of its forces, the parallel increase of its *usefulness and docility*, its integration into systems of efficient and economic controls, all this was ensured by the procedures of power that characterised the *disciplines*: an *anatomo-politics of the human body*.
> The second, formed somewhat later, focussed on *the species body*, the body imbued with the mechanics of life and serving as the basis of the biological processes: propagation, births and mortality, the level of health, life expectancy and longevity, with all the conditions that can cause them to vary. Their supervision was effected through an entire series of interventions and *regulatory controls: a bio-politics of the population*. (Foucault, 1980a, p. 139; altered for my emphasis)

The double reduction of administrable bodies, from the inside and the outside, constitutes a major advance in the history of the power of all administrative bodies. The benefit of Foucault's archaeologies of these bodily histories is to recover the natural history of the production of the docility, utility and governmentability of the social body. This embodied history tends to disappear from the abstract process of rationalization which we shall consider in the Parsons/Weber scheme. Parsons's abstracted reading of Durkheim, Weber and even Freud permits the pattern variable code to operate by taking for granted the history of the production of docility described by Foucault and Marx. The disciplinary culture required to produce factory labor, to urbanize it, to render it minimally literate, to check crime and disease and to evolve some common standards of public health, hygiene and safety presented huge problems, and even today it still faces resistance and sabotage.

It is important to see how Foucault's diagnosis of the spread of bio-power throughout the social body, its regulation of physical, moral, mental conduct, its measurements and comparative rankings, its examinations, records and constant surveillance render obsolete any account of the operation of power as the agency of the juridico-legal subject, as in liberalism, or as a repressive mechanism as in Freudo-Marxist theory. Bio-power regulates bodies individually, as in the clinical model, and collectively, as on the model of social medicine. The two strategies are combined to produce the most complete system of discipline ever known in the history of power. Disciplinary power works in hospitals, schools, prisons, armies, factories and bureaucracies. It is compatible with shifting vocabularies of rights, reform and welfare. It is intimate and collective; it is obeyed not because of its power over death but because of its power over life. It is this shift in emphasis that is the source of the expansion of bio-power whose corresponding apparatus we may call the *therapeutic state*.

From the idea that the state has its own nature and its own finality, to the idea that man is the true object of the state's power, as far as he produces a surplus strength, as far as he is a living, working, speaking being, as far as he constitutes a society, and as far as he belongs to a population in an environment, we can see the increasing intervention of the state in the life of the individual. The importance of life for their problems of political power increases; a kind of animalisation of man through the most sophisticated techniques results. Both the development of the possibilities of the human and social sciences, and the simultaneous possibility of protecting life and of the holocaust make their historical appearance. (Foucault, Lecture at Stanford University, October 1974, cited in Dreyfus and Rabinow, 1983, p. 138)

Foucault's conception of *disciplinary technology* includes not only punishment and prison but innumerable strategies for the division measurement, dressage and diagnosis of bodily, emotional and mental operations which can be attached to a whole range of institutional sites, from the clinic to the school, army, hospital, factory to modern bureaucracies and their administration of computerized dossiers. Here we have the field for the behavioral and social sciences, the raw data, the right to interview, to record, to cross-check, to observe and generally to enmesh the individual in documentary histories and programs which weave together intimacy and the therapeutic policy. Here the individual is subjected to the knowable community administered by the social science disciplines. The latter are created *pari passu* with the very social science anomalies – the idle, insane, pervert, criminal, ignorant – they are designed to remove. Thus, the normalization and abnormalization of processes in the individual and social body are two sides of a single practice which continuously expands the social sciences as administrative disciplines in the therapeutic society.

The Parsonian Physician

We need a more focal image than that of 'crisis' to convey the relation between sociology and the therapeutic society which it administers. Let us speak of *sociological nemesis*, borrowing from Ivan Illich's (1978) thesis on the iatrogenic, that is, medically self-induced, problems of medical practice. Much of the self-criticism of sociological practice is concerned with its own debilitating effects upon individual agency, its reinforcement of state institutional dependency and its exaggerated confidence in the powers of a therapeutic society to hold together individuals without bonds of intimacy towards anyone else than themselves (Rieff, 1966). Sociologists have deplored collectivism, aggressive individualism, alienation, anomie, affluence, poverty, family breakdown, mental illness, crime, deviance and every form of sociological theory and practice except their own brand. Indeed, sociologists have so successfully deplored their own practice that they no longer have a professional monopoly upon their complaints. The vocabulary of the social sciences was never very far from ordinary language to begin with but due to widespread teaching and media usage everyone has a vernacular sociology sophisticated enough to include sociology itself as part of the troubles of modern society. Indeed, this is the more general effect of modern knowledge. The more we know about economics, psychoanalysis, medicine and meteorology, the more we are plagued with their troubles in exchange for their panaceas.

The professionalization of bio-power in the agencies of social welfare with the concomitant mixing of law, psychoanalysis and medicine in the treatment and administration of the poor, mentally ill, criminal, handicapped and retarded is the medium in which the Parsonian sociologist is the more happily employed the worse things get – hence 'the crisis of opportunity'.

Although in practice Parsons is aware of this context of sociological employment, at the theoretical level he never grasped the nature of bio-power as the apparatus which spreads with the help of the Parsonian discursive strategy of producing a theory of social control on the therapeutic model of the reduction of deviance to illness. This strategy is, of course, rhetorically suited to the liberal, humanist concern with individualized troubles and to a professional, physician-like response to the troubled society which calls for the practice of sociology and psychoanalysis. For the rest, Parsons (1967) remained attached to the utilitarian concept of power as a symbolic medium of exchange functioning according to the principles of the money market. This obliged Parsons to treat all the dysfunctions of power, property, stratification, status and professionalism as 'strains' in the system. Interestingly enough, the very metaphor of 'strain' in turn invites professional medical or engineering correction.

We need now to consider how sociology fashioned itself for the physician role in the therapeutic society. This, I think, is the enduring achievement of Parsonian theory (O'Neill, 1976), though, of course, there are precedents in Plato, Durkheim and Freud, to name a few. At the same time, we do not mean to overlook that the Parsonian codification of the relevant behaviors productive of social control abstracts from the history of violence focused by Foucault's studies of bio-power. The Parsonian code presupposes this history of violence. It presumes that the production of docility is now largely a task at the attitudinal level, a matter of cognitive orientation. This makes it much easier to think of *the citizen as a patient*, rather than to face the able-bodied worker, unionized and politicized to fight against the system, to renegotiate its terms without the temptation to conceal himself as a deviant or sick entity in the social body. Parsonian discourse concretizes (despite its own abstraction) the disciplinary practices of sociology as a para-medical aim of the therapeutic administration of docile citizens. Parsons (1978, p. 18) makes it quite clear that he conceived the sick role and the role of the therapeutic agent (doctor, psychoanalyst, social worker) in the framework of *social control*. In other words, health and illness were thought of as patterns of motivation towards the social system, of commitment in the 'normal' case and of withdrawal in the deviant case – the complication arising that illness might excuse withdrawal or faulting of the social system:

I should regard deviance and social control as phenomena concerned with the integrative problems of a social system. Illness we may speak of as, at least in one primary aspect, an impairment of the sick person's integration in solitary relationship with others, in family, jobs, and many other contexts. Seen in this perspective, therapy may be interpreted to be predominantly a reintegrative process. To be successful, such a process must take account of adaptive considerations, notably the pathological state of the organism and/or personality and the nature of the patient's adaptive problems in various aspects of his or her life. (Parsons, 1978, p. 20)

Parsons's standpoint should not be taken naïvely. Every social system must fulfill the task of mobilizing the loyalty of its citizens, the energy of its work force and the reproductive will of its families. Sometimes these commitments are considered restrictive. Yet, as Freud observed with respect to the incest taboo, the law is there not because we never break it but precisely because we do. Instincts, in other words, are social achievements, owing their second nature to the laws that invoke them. Every social system rests upon sanctions of reward and punishment which are written into the hearts and minds of its members. The punitive order in modern societies is tied to conditional love at the level of the individual psychic system – mediated by the family – and to the differential reward of power, status and economic opportunity at the level of class system. Such arrangements form the quasi-natural environment in which individuals are motivated to acquire the ordinary competences, skills, values and aversions that constitute the normal, able-bodied citizen. Because much can go wrong in the interaction between individuals, families, classes and the social system, society is obliged to find interpretive codes for dealing with sin, rebellion, alientation, illness, retreatism, anomie, narcissism and the like. For this reason, all societies institutionalize therapeutic practices – magic, religion, ethics, art and the human sciences – whose function is to reconcile individual and collective life. Broadly speaking, godlessness, illness, crime and rebellion are most feared by the institutions of legitimate order since their monopoly of knowledge, values and force is best exercised as rarely as possible if it is to have maximum demonstration effect.

Parsons assigns the social control function of medicine to the necessary features of its *fiduciary* place in a society that values health over illness and relevant scientific knowledge and training over ignorance. These features entail an unavoidable asymmetric relation between the professional and the layperson, putting a strain upon trust, the right to consent, participation and such values that favor individualism in open compensation. Any radical questioning of the 'professional complex' would threaten modern society with regressive de-differentiation, pushing the open society based upon rationalized professionalism into tribalism and ignorance.

Like other professional roles, that of the physician may be categorised in pattern variable terms. It has a high incidence of universalistic standards, for example, of the generalisability of propositions about diagnosis and probable therapeutic consequences of medical measures. It is functionally specific in that the relations of physicians to their patients are focused on problems of the patients' health rather than on other sorts of personal problems. It is performance oriented in that the task of the physician is to intervene actively in actual cares of illness and its threat, not to sit passively by and 'let nature take its course.' It is also predominantly affectively neutral, though with the kinds of qualifications that Renee Fox ... has proposed under her concept of 'detached concern'. Finally, by contrast with the entrepreneur or executive, the professional role generally, including that of the physician, is governed by an orientation towards collective values. The most-central manifestation of this is the professional ideology that puts the welfare of the patient ahead of the self interest of the therapeutic agents, physicians in particular. (Parsons, 1978, p. 75)

The Parsonian Patient

The point of intersection between the individual bio-psychic system and the socio-cultural system lies in his/her individual role-performance (Parsons, 1951). It is here that we find the motivational switchpoint through which the individual channels commitment or alienation, health or illness, normalcy or deviance. It is, in other words, the focal point of social control. Consider the Parsonian Table on page 30.

Because the social system can 'ordinarily' expect individuals to conform to its beliefs and values with the production of institutionally and situationally appropriate conduct (as well as age, gender and role-specific attributes), as a result of shared culture and familization (socialization) society is able to forgo the extraordinarily punitive sanctions of the social system. This is not to say that individuals fail to question the religious and moral norms of their society, to query the justice of its stratification, or to question its age and gender structures. Clearly, all of this happens. But the bias of the official society is to treat such conduct as deviant, criminal or sick and rarely to concede that rejections of the system may be legitimately political or spiritual motivations. In this regard, churches, universities, political parties and the state all exhibit a similar bias towards social control. On the individual level the consequences of social alienation are scenic – poverty, ignorance, ugliness, punishment, confinement and possible execution. Thus, individuals are expected to 'see for themselves' the lesson that is before their very eyes, namely, that in our society it is better to succeed than to fail.

Table 1.1

	Disturbance of total person	Disturbance of particular expectations
'Situational' focus	Problem of 'capacities' for task role performance	Problem of commitments to collectivities (Barnard's 'efficiency')
	Illness as deviance Health as 'conformity'	Disloyalty as deviance Loyalty as conformity
'Normative' focus	Problem of commitments to values, or of 'morality' 'Sin' and 'immorality' as deviance	Problem of commitments to norms, or of 'legality' 'Crime' and 'illegality' as deviance
	State of grace or 'good character' as conformity	Law-observance as conformity

Source: Talcott Parsons, 'Definitions of Health and Illness in the Light of American Values and Social Structure' in E. Gartly Jaco (ed.), _Patients, physicians and Illness: sourcebook in behavioral science and medicine_, 1974, Free Press, Glencoe, Ill., copyright © 1958; table quoted by permission of The Free Press, a Division of Macmillan, Inc.

Moreover, they are expected to moralize on this lesson as a matter of individual motivation to succeed and to avoid failure and not to inquire about alternative social systems that might motivate individuals in other directions. We owe to R. K. Merton (1938) the classical formulation of the options that face the individual in the choice of social commitment or social alienation. The Parsons–Merton formulations of deviance are clear enough in their endorsement of the bias toward social order as a 'generalized' social system requirement. But whereas in the Mertonian vision, as Stinchcombe (1975, p. 31) remarks, 'we are not quite sure that hollow conformity to a manifest function is exactly the same as hollow ritualism of the lower middle class', in Parsons there is a more optimistic presumption that the medicalization of the socio-psychic costs of social control will push the social system along its determined path of rationalized modernity.

I suggest, then, that the American pattern of illness is focussed on the problem of capacity for achievement for the individual person. Therapeutically, recovery is defined for him as a _job_ to be done in cooperation with those who are technically qualified to help him. This focus then operates to polarise the components of the 'problem' in such a way that _the primary threat to his achievement capacity which must be_ *overcome is dependency.* The element of exemption from ordinary role-obligations may then be interpreted as permissiveness for temporary relief from the strains of trying hard to achieve. The patient is permitted to indulge his dependency needs under strictly regulated conditions, notably his recognition of the conditional nature of the legitimacy of his state, and exposure to the therapeutic task. (Parsons, 1965, pp. 286–7; original emphasis)

Parsons's social system is a cuckoo's nest. If working on behalf of the system makes the individual ill, he or she may become sick provided one works at getting well enough to risk getting ill again. Catch-22 is that the disciplinary code summarized in the pattern variables makes health and illness two sides of the same coin, two dimensions of rationalized conduct subservient to the professional complex. At the social system level, the American value placed upon 'health' is required, as Parsons recognizes, because rationalized society cannot tolerate pre-industrial levels of mental pathology, nor can the nuclear family manage the increased load of 'personality management' required for commitment to the achievement society. Given the American bias toward self-commitment rather than collective indoctrination, stress is exerted upon the individual to produce attitudes and behavior compliant with the American way of life and to self-fault rather than blame the social system for one's failure to conform. Thus, deviance, ritualism and illness are the institutionally channeled motivations of the weak and underprivileged in American society. In the absence of alternative political vocabularies of motivation, the social system will be disposed to merge illness and deviance according to the medical model of social control, as Parsons concedes:

It is not meant to press the similarity between psychotherapy and other mechanisms of social control too far. Certainly there are just as important differences as there are similarities, but the relationship seems to be sufficiently close, and the common factors sufficiently general, so that then similarities can provide important leads to the recognition and analysis of the operation of control mechanisms which as such are by no means obvious to common sense ... An immense amount of research will be necessary in this fold. (Parsons, 1951, p. 319)

Medicalization of Society

Parsons, then, is not only a pioneer in the field of medical sociology. He is a pioneer in *the medicalization of sociology* as a professionalized agency of social control. The enormous costs of modern medicine in all its forms arouse public concern not simply because of fiscal overload but precisely because of the danger of inflating the costs of social control. While it is true that traditional societies surrender a fair amount of their social surplus to religious and military expenditures, it is ironic that it is more likely that modern society will overcharge itself for social control combined with military extravaganzas. However, the more immediate issue remains the ability of the American social system to buy off the human destruction and disablement created by its class and property system without espousing 'socialized' health and medical care, not to mention other charges to the economic system. Thus, it was particularly challenging for Parsons to sociologize the medical institutions in keeping with the pattern-variable formulation of professionalism on the physician side and the will to independent achievement on the patient side, with permissive relations strictly controlled to ensure the patient's re-integration into the social system. For this achievement Parsons can be said to have moved sociology in second place to medicine in the aristocracy of the occupational world.

This process in turn has been associated with an extension of the focus of ultimate 'responsibility' for the health problems of the society. There was once a sense in which the medical profession shouldered that responsibility virtually unaided except for the basic legitimation of its position in the community. Now it clearly must be shared with administration and trustees, governmental and private, and with universities or organisations. Perhaps above all it is now shared with the various relevant scientific professions, the most recent additions to which are the behavioral. (Parsons, 1965, p. 355)

Rather than engage any further in the polemics of Parsonianism, we propose now to return to the work of Michel Foucault in as much as it permits us to understand the discursive production of Parsonian–Weberian sociology as a *disciplinary code* which integrates sociological theory and its professional practice with the administration of a rationalized society. The affinity between the medical model and the social control model is a discursive achievement of Parsons which makes sociology a focal discipline in the complex of power/knowledge that administers modern therapeutic society. It translates the problem of the punitive order into a health problem, with positive sanctions awarded to social commitment, and a secondary system of positive reinforcement awarded to compliance with the sickness/deviance system as a reintegrative mechanism aligned with individualized competitive achievement. As such, the Parsonian code is a sub-strategy within a larger historical shift in the exercise of political power as a theater of cruelty exercised through extreme torture, execution or cruel confinement, to power exercised as knowledge generalized by the human sciences. This is the wider canvas of the medicalization of the social sciences, as well as of the sociologization of the medical sciences. To a certain extent both Parsons and Foucault may be said to share the medical model of the social sciences. Foucault, of course, goes much further than Parsons in the direction of a deconstruction of the medical codes and the disciplinary matrix in which they reside. Moreover, Foucault understands that interpretative analysis cannot presume upon the externalized stance of science. The physician, analyst and sociologist are not free subjects in the production of the practices of subjectification/ objectification which bind knowledge/power. The social scientist has no universal voice. He or she practices within the professional complex that articulates the therapeutic state to the individuals bound to it by rights to health, education and employment. By the same token, we cannot make the assumption that the neo-Keynesian economy has absorbed class conflict into consumerism and its discontents, with mental and physical health offered as a free public good evincing the social system's ultimate respect for life. Although there is much about the therapeutic society to render this view plausible, it is best not to lose sight of Marx's insistence upon a constantly revised sociology of the industrialization process. Thus, it is necessary to retain Marx's research principle which instructs us to look for the next stage in the drive of capitalism to replace human beings with machines.

We might then call the present phase of late capitalism the stage of *bio-technological capitalism*. We refer to the increasing replacement of the internal body by *prosthetic technologies* – if not by totally engineered biograms – and to the simultaneous reshaping of collective life by de-anthropomorphizing institutions (O'Neill, 1985) among which, curiously enough, the therapeutic complex, including the social and behavioral sciences, plays a huge role. Thus, the medical model, however updated in its bio-technological phase, remains subservient to the reproduction of capitalist relations of production in which alienation, occupational diseases and environmental hazards are the principal sources of impoverished health. Modern medicine nevertheless remains individual-ized, technologized and symptomatic. At the same time, medicine reproduces its own place in that aristocracy of the occupational world, as Parsons calls it, to which social scientists aspire. It does not contradict this observation to find that medicine and the social services, despite their individualist ideology and practice, are increasingly state funded. This is because the therapeutic role of the state in late capitalism is to meet the social needs created/ignored by the processes of capital accumulation. The fiscal 'crisis' of the modern state is all the more 'naturally' expressed through the medical metaphor of 'crisis' in as much as the medical and therapeutic services of the state are constantly faced with alternating expansions and cutbacks. These fluctuations in turn send chills and fevers through the medicalized social sciences. By the same token, sociological self-interest and the voice of social conscience are nicely blended. Thus the professions suffer from depression and elation; their hopes rise and fall with those of the rest of society whose moods they otherwise administer.

Can the social physicians cure themselves? Once the question is raised, it services a host of remedies. Abandon the subject, adopt anti-realism, go holistic, retribalize, restore folk and feminized medicine. Ironicize, stoicize, politicize – the dream of universal knowledge is over. The mind is an armed camp and not an open school. The sickness of the civilized animal is incurable, however fine its interim therapies. What is to be done? Illich says that he deliberately chose to speak of medical *nemesis* in order to underline that the self-induced troubles of our medicalized culture are not on the same level as the troubles it seeks to remedy. We have chosen to speak of *sociological nemesis* for the same reason. Nemesis is a response to mankind's *hubris* in trying to step outside of itself – into a divinity, to play the philosopher-king, the political physician, or transcendental analyst.

By using the Greek [*nemesis*] I want to emphasise that the corresponding phenomenon does not fit within the explanatory paradigm now offered by bureaucrats, therapists, and ideologues for the snowballing diseconomies and disutilities that, lacking all intuition, they have engineered and that they tend to call the 'counterintuitive' behavior of large systems. By invoking the myths and ancestral gods I should make it clear that my framework for analysis of the current breakdown of medicine is foreign to the industrially determined logic and ethos. (Illich, 1978, pp. 43–4)

There is no intention here of recommending what Paul Starr (1982) calls 'therapeutic nihilism' with respect to either medical or sociological practice. The issues are far too complex for such a response. It cannot be denied that medicine, education and criminal rehabilitation serve social control functions aided by the social sciences which in turn expropriate the central metaphors (above all, 'crisis') of medicine, law and therapy. This cycle serves to expand governmental intervention, itself formulated in the same discursive formats whose production it finds in policy research. Whether the wheel of government turns faster or slower, the individual is still caught inside, over-treated or under-treated by the therapeutic state. Conservatives will want to off-load onto the private sector, invoking the family and individual practice in a world from which both are disappearing. Socialists of any stripe will prefer to call for more public provision even though the therapeutic sciences and allied agencies cannot deliver their promise. In effect the most likely outcome, as Starr predicts, is that rationalization will be effected through the corporate organization of the medical complex and, we may add, its client social sciences. This will pre-empt public policy just as surely as it will trade up the stratification scale, leaving the poor outside of the preferred practice of the health and therapy they may want, and neglecting the services they in fact need due to the lives they lead in this social system.

Conclusion: Sociology as a Skin Trade

In other writings (O'Neill, 1972, 1985) I have set out a rival conception of the *embodied subject* who suffers the hopes and defeats of what I have called 'sociology as a skin trade'. At the same time I began to renovate the imagery of society as a *body-politic*, to differentiate the levels of the *bio-body*, the *productive body* and the *libidinal body* as sites where human beings pursue the relevant knowledge and values of health, work and happiness. Each level of discourse requires the formulation of relevant technical knowledge (medicine, political economy, sociology and psychoanalysis) and each level has its own emancipatory discourse about health creativity and self-expression. Because each of these discursive interests is likely to be articulated by professional social scientists and therapists, it is necessary to require the institutionalization of mechanisms of political and ethical accountability to laypersons' common-sense knowledge and values regarding their bodies, their families, their work and their souls. Medical and sociological nemesis is not the result of a therapeutic conspiracy against society. It belongs to the radical technological *a priori* of Western knowledge whose ambition is fundamentally *bio-technological*. The sin of Adam and Eve was the best humankind could manage at the time. In today's laboratory Adam and Eve can be bypassed and life can be set in motion according to the best genetic formulas. Huge legal, ethical and sociological problems are simultaneously generated. And thus we step into a new 'crisis of opportunity' for which very few social scientists are prepared – whether by training or morals.

2

Sociological Theory and Practical Reason: the Restriction of the Scope of Sociological Theory

Nico Stehr

The history of sociological theory has seen repeated efforts by sociologists to purge sociological discourse of a wide range of considerations deemed extraneous. Politics, ethics, philosophy, epistemology and history, representing concerns which in many ways predate but also gave rise to sociology, are now seen to have their own separate 'professional' identities, as does, of course, sociology itself.[1] The growing specialization and differentiation of scientific discourse provides the social basis for the very possibility of increasingly restricted modes of discourse. But sociological discourse is not merely either a passive beneficiary or a victim of these developments. As a matter of fact, much of sociology aspires to and celebrates its intellectual self-sufficiency and self-restriction.

In this essay, I will argue that contemporary sociology might well be better off if it does not restrict its boundaries of permissible discourse as severely as it often does, and returns to the broader range of concerns characteristic of 'classical sociological theory'. By this I do not mean to suggest that exactly the same leading assumptions, similar theoretical intentions, an identical vocabulary, or the methods of classical sociology should be the foundation of modern sociology. But I do mean to suggest that modern sociology should be able to learn from the success of classical sociology – a success based on an expansive conception of its own limits.

Rationalization and Sociology

When Talcott Parsons (1937, p. 3) in *The Structure of Social Action* asked the rhetorical question first posed by Crane Brinton (1933, pp. 226–7),

'Who now reads Spencer?', he intended thereby to advance a particular historiography of social science. The 'working hypothesis' of Parson's reconstruction of sociological theory consequently was that an immanent (intellectual) development was taking place in social theory which had significantly diminished the value of Spencer's contribution by the time of Parson's own *The Structure of Social Action*. Herbert Spencer, as the typical representative of the later stages of development of the positivistic–utilitarian tradition, was himself 'the victim of the vengeance of the jealous god, Evolution, in this case the evolution of scientific theory'.[2] The direction of this process of immanent development was characterized by Parsons (1937, pp. 12–13) as development toward a form of theoretical discourse in which adequacy was a 'matter of the logical exigencies of theoretical systems in close mutual interrelation with observations of empirical fact and general statements embodying these facts'.

Contemporary sociologists see their discipline increasingly in terms of and subject to the process Parsons describes but especially on the basis of the often largely implicit notion that such immanent development of science necessarily produces a more distinct, differentiated scientific version of theory in sociology.[3] Such a distinct mode of discourse, one is allowed to infer from Parsons's observation, is one that increasingly obeys immanent laws of 'internal' development (thus is not very much if at all affected by external social factors). It produces a common body of ideas despite diverse extraneous intellectual influence, and frees itself successively from intellectual issues and empirical concerns to which other scientific theories legitimately have to attend.

This is a curiously narrow perspective. The history of social thought has seen the emergence of a wide range of epistemological positions, conceptual structures, theories of society (and even political programs associated with them). But the prevailing historiography of sociology interprets this history as a process of increasing convergence and proper restriction of the sociological tradition. The predominant history of sociology describes this process also as one of emancipation, consolidation and synthesis of the discipline which insures, at least at some future date, scientific maturity, exemplified, for example, in the observation and admonition that 'sociology has already had a history of severing some of its connections with social philosophy, social policy, social problems, and social ideology ... and it may be correct to view the future of sociology as one of spinning off some frameworks and consolidating those that remain' (Smelser, 1969, p. 6; also, Lipset and Smelser, 1961; Parsons, 1961).[4]

The use of this image of development through differentiation and rationalization indicates that sociology is seen by its major intellectual historians and advocates as self-exemplifying. The rationalization of modern society finds its counterpart in the effort to rationalize sociology. The elimination of ethical and political concerns from sociological discourse would then coincide with developments that rid modern society itself of ethical and political 'problems' (cf. Habermas, 1974, pp. 1–81; Hirschman, 1983, pp. 24–9).

Positive Sociological Discourse

The predominant historiography of sociology thus converges toward the advocacy and often the celebration of what might be called *positive sociological discourse*, that is, a form and a scope of discourse for sociology which recognizes and scrupulously observes, as Parsons (1968, p. 321) has formulated it, a 'meaningful intellectual division of ideas' among social scientific disciplines.[5] A positive mode of discourse, as Neal Smelser (1969, p. 16) has advocated and tautologically described it, is one in which ' no investigative activity in sociology is scientifically legitimate unless it can be related directly to the core sociological enterprise: accounting for variations and interdependencies of data within a sociological framework'.

Positive sociological discourse, therefore, is sociological discourse in the narrow sense of the term sociology; sociologists have succeeded in differentiating it from problems which at one time were seen to be very much part of sociological discourse. Among them are philosophical–epistemological questions and moral–political issues. The latter, it is argued, are external to the domain of positive sociological discourse, while the former set of questions is part of the autonomous discipline of philosophy or the philosophy of science. A kind of contempt for the various sciences vis-à-vis one another and vis-à-vis common sense or practical reason has been a consequence of this process (cf. Mannheim, 1940, p. 29).

It is not my intention to question, at one level, the autonomy from extraneous social and intellectual constraints of the different sciences as they may have emerged historically. The social and intellectual differentation among disciplines need not, perhaps cannot, be reversed. Autonomy, even in the social sciences, is and can at times be considerable, particularly in the case of empirical social research. But at another level, in particular at the level of the formation of theory, the basic and necessary interconnectedness of sociological, moral and epistemological issues cannot be ignored (cf. Tejera, 1979, p. 193). At the point of the formation of theory, that is at the level of the generation of meaning-structures, such interdependence is not only inescapable, but provides for the very possibility of discourse and ultimately assures that the special social sciences attain specific relevance for other societal institutions.

The quest for an objective and positive sociological mode of discourse is strongly linked to the aspiration for scientific maturity and unity. This commitment is without question also a particular moral commitment, strongly associated with the hope of 'dissolving the differences that divide and the distances that operate even by uniting them in a single peace-bringing version of the world' (Gouldner, 1973, p. 66). The ethics of a commitment for unity, for objectivity through consensus, in short, for maturity based on convergence and communality motivates the effort to 'fit the partial and broken fragments together; to provide a picture that transcends the nagging sense of incompleteness; to overcome the multiplicity of shifting perspectives' (Gouldner, 1973, p. 66).[6]

The search for intellectual unity and maturity in sociology coincides, moreover, with crucial features of the social organization of the scientific community, in particular, with the organizing principle of science – the elimination of disagreement. And this makes for a paradox. Dispassionate and disinterested discourse, it is argued, requires autonomy; objectivity is the main reason for the intellectual power of discourse (cf. Toulmin, 1976b); and restriction is seen as the distinguishing mark of objectivity. Objectivity achieved in this manner must, it is presumed, put an end to troubling and persistent disagreement among sociologists. In short, to the extent that sociologists have succeeded in purging sociological discourse of moral, political, philosophical and epistemological questions, they are seen as assuring the objective (scientific), effective (useful), and consensual (truthful) character of sociological discourse. But the consequent restriction in the scope of sociological theory embodied in this quest for positive discourse not only limits the political relevance of sociological knowledge, it is also based on a simplistic and reductionist model of human action which further reinforces its own limits. A *homo sociologicus* is as limited as the *homo economicus* of much of economic theory.[7]

Ethics, Epistemology and Sociological Discourse

The severing of practical reasoning (ethics) from science and the severing of philosophy (epistemology) from the special sciences occur at different times. The most important moment in the process came as philosophers, searching for an explanation of the great success of Galilean science, whose discoveries were so much more powerful than those of Aristotle, concluded upon examining the language of Galilean science that 'the more metaphysically comfortless and morally insignificant our vocabulary, the more likely we are to be "in touch with reality" or to be "scientific" or to describe reality as it wants to be described and thereby get it under control' (Rorty, 1983, p. 158). Thus, to eliminate from scientific discourse any terminology which is endowed with social purposes results in a vocabulary, it was argued, which is close or identical to that of nature itself. In the case of the social sciences this powerful notion converges, at a later time, with efforts to secure an autonomous and distinct discourse in social science. In many instances these efforts took the form of emulating the natural sciences, and rejecting classical sociological theory.

Where the purpose of classical sociological discourse was in part to create moral relevance or to respond to urgent public issues, the aim of these later efforts was to stay aloof from moral vocabularies, from epistemological inquiries, and from immediate practical matters (cf. Stehr and Meja, 1985). Epistemological questions have not been entirely eliminated from scientific discourse but instead are seen largely as belonging to fields other than the special sciences. For sociology, this implies that a sociology of scientific knowledge which does not limit itself to a sociology of scientific organization, but attempts to discuss the origin, construction and validation of knowledge claims, is improper.

To be sure, neither the boundaries with ethics nor the boundaries with epistemology have been stable. The lengthy discussion and advocacy of value-neutrality in sociology is only the most visible side of the struggle to legitimate a sharp demarcation between moral–political and sociological questions. Attempts to demarcate epistemology and sociology have been equally ardent (cf. Gieryn, 1983),[8] but recently this boundary too has been unsettled, especially as a consequence of the rise of 'constructivist' sociologies of science.

Interdependence of Epistemology, Ethics and Sociology

Despite announcements, at various times in the past, that sociology has or is about to show the characteristics of mature science, positive sociological discourse has had few of the cognitive successes that are the mark of 'maturity'. This poor track record does not necessarily mean that the quest for a positive sociology is doomed. The failures can be excused by the claim that this discourse is undertaken under 'adverse' circumstances; that is, that the necessary prerequisites, both within the scientific community and in society at large, simply do not yet exist. This excuse amounts to a confession that despite the self-conception of advocates of such discourse, the genesis of positive sociological discourse depends on external circumstances – the clash of world-views, fundamental differences in interests of diverse strata or entrenched forms of social and economic inequality within as well as among nations, do not favor positive sociological discourse.[9] Making this concession does not alter the ideal of positive discourse in sociology, but pushes the hope for its realization into the distant future.

In this future, positive discourse may well monopolize, and therefore end the contemporary diversity of, sociology. But this historical possibility does not imply the desirability of positive sociological discourse. Yet any determined effort to entrench positive discourse in sociology is from the beginning linked to convictions about its desirability, and especially about the social and intellectual benefits of positive discourse of the discipline and society at large. Thus, even in the case of this question, the necessary interdependence of epistemology, ethics and sociology becomes evident.

Indeed, the conclusion that positive sociological discourse is possible rests on the very notion which reduces the same epistemology program to one among various potential conceptions. Using Max Weber's language (although his position is by no means unique in this regard), the transcendental presupposition of the socio-historical sciences is the existence of 'historischen Individuen' (1951, p. 180), historically individual or 'unique' cases. Social scientists are, like their subjects, persons shaped by unique socio-historical circumstances. As such, they can never transcend the object of their investigation. Yet positive social science is an attempt to seek the universal, an attempt to achieve just this impossibility.

The paradox is especially evident with respect to culture. The social sciences must, as Weber argues in his 'Objectivity' essay, draw on, respond to, and be limited by those patterns of meaning entrenched in our culture. Culture is 'meaningful', endowed with human purposes. The success of social science, if it is to be successful at all, depends on the extent to which its meaning structures resonate with those found in the culture generally. The meaning structures which are constitutive for society are, as Weber has argued as well, most diverse but also morally compelling. The variety of meaning structures makes the application of a singular structure not impossible but trivial or even false, if not positively undesirable (cf. Louch, 1966, p. 208).

Paralleling these epistemological paradoxes is an ethical paradox. If one assumes, as Norbert Elias has done recently, that social scientists are confronted with problems which derive from dual membership in communities, some of which function primarily on the basis of considerations of practical reason and one of which – the community of social science – functions primarily on the basis of the aim of advancing social scientific reason, this problem

cannot simply be solved by the social scientists relinquishing their function as members of their group in favor of their functions as scientists. They cannot stop taking part in the social and political matters of their group and their time, they cannot avoid being concerned by them. Moreover, their own participation, their engagement, is one of the prerequisites for understanding the problems they will have to solve in their capacity as scientists. You do not need to know what it is like to be an atom in order to be able to understand the structure of a molecule but it is absolutely necessary to know as an insider how people experience their own and other groups in order to understand how human groups function; this cannot be understood without active participation and engagement. (Elias, 1983, p. 30; my translation)

Even the strongest proponents of positive sociological discourse concede that 'sociological theory borders very closely on logic and epistemology, as moral and political philosophy' (Smelser, 1969, p. 16). These paradoxes show something more: that sociology can never be 'autonomous'. This inherent limitation does not mean that sociology ought to replace or be replaced by epistemology or ethics. But it does imply that sociology is by no means at liberty to advance just any point of view, for what applies to its object is equally relevant to itself. 'Men make their own history, but they do not make it just as they please' (Marx, 1965a, p. 15).

Notes

1 These disciplines have indeed become increasingly autonomous. For example, anyone familiar with the contemporary literature on the philosophical foundations of ethics – say, from John Rawls's *A Theory of Justice* up to Alan Donagan's *Theory of Morality* and Ronald Dworkin's *Taking Rights Seriously* – will know how little attention such books give to 'science', or at least to 'natural and social sciences'. See Derrida, 1982, p. 148, and Toulmin, 1976a, p. 403.

2 The language of *The Structure of Social Action* is in many respects the language of the texts it sets out to analyze in detail, i.e. classical sociological thought. Thus, this early work of Parsons is itself a product of classical sociological theory; cf. Stehr and Meja, 1985. More specifically, the phrase 'the vengeance of the jealous god, Evolution' in the sentence quoted is a note on language in sociology which signifies that Parsons had not yet succeeded in 'neutralizing' its referents.

3 For Talcott Parsons, 1937, pp. 13–14, the distinctiveness of sociological theory at the beginning of this century begins to emerge in the work of Durkheim, Pareto, Marshall and Weber, who despite their different social and intellectual backgrounds and effects on the general 'climate of opinion', all worked on and developed a *common* body of ideas.

4 The increasing restriction in the scope of sociology has, however, different consequences than the same differentiation from other specialities for those social science fields which are 'associated' with distinct societal institutions, as is the case for law, economics and perhaps political science; cf. Claessens, 1966. For example, the 'correspondence' between at least the economic system and economics minimizes the danger that economic thought will become substantially irrelevant, although the possibility of knowledge production in economics which is mainly self-referential is also present. In general, sociology lacks a corresponding societal sub-system as a referent or client and therefore is

subject to accelerated insulation once the discipline reaches a critical size, as is the case at the present time.

5 In a review of Alexander von Schelting's *Max Webers Wissenschaftslehre*, published in 1936, Talcott Parsons describes a *positive* sociology of knowledge approvingly as one which concentrates exclusively on sociological analyses of knowledge and therefore is legislated to refrain from any interest in what are properly epistemological and philosophical issues. See Parsons, 1936b, p. 680; cf. also Stehr and Meja, 1982.

6 As Gouldner, 1973, p. 67, also warns, and what is perhaps more discrediting to this kind of quest for objectivity and for human unity, is that 'since its [sociology's] classical formulation, its most gifted spokesmen have often had totalitarian proclivities; they came to be viewed as enemies of the "open society", who denied the value and reality of human difference'.

7 Albert O. Hirschman advocates a concern with morality *in* social science discourse; however, he is opposed to morality *for* social science discourse. For Hirschman, 1983, p. 29, moral issues need to become a 'variable' in economic discourse. 'What is needed is for economists to incorporate into their analyses, whenever that is pertinent, such basic traits and emotions as the desire for power and for sacrifice, the fear of boredom, pleasure in both commitment and unpredictability, the search of meaning and community, and so on.'

8 The collision of and vigorous efforts toward a separation of sociological and epistemological issues in the case of sociology can best be observed in the specialities of the sociology of science and knowledge. See, for example, Berger and Luckmann, 1967; Stark, 1958; von Schelting, 1934.

9 Compare Stehr, 1979, for an analysis and framework of some of the factors which reproduce diverse discourse in sociology.

3

State, Ethics and Public Morality in American Sociological Thought

Arthur J. Vidich and Stanford M. Lyman

From the beginning, sociological thought in the United States had its roots in the Protestant religion. The emergence of secular thought itself may be seen as a penetration of civil society by religious values. The development of two social science traditions, pragmatism and function- alism, bears on a set of intellectual and moral dilemmas common to both theology and sociology, especially when each seeks to define a public philosophy. The interest of America's philosophical pragmatists in the moral groundings of society, and particularly in the process by which the religious authority of Puritanism had been lost in the general movement toward secularization, was always explicit. In contrast, functionalists have assumed that society already had a moral grounding, and focus attention on the working out of that morality within social, political and economic institutions.

Situated Ethics in an Amoral Society

Pragmatic thought had its beginnings in the work of Josiah Royce (1885–1916), who sought to uplift American society from its descent into amoral chaos and transform it into a veritable respiritualized national community. In the lineage of thought about this transformation that descends from Royce to Mead to Blumer and to Goffman, the singular and binding communitarian covenant of the Protestant ethicists erodes in the face of the emergence of a plurality of worldly, non-binding, situational and personal ethics. In place of the unified moral community, there appears the multitude of individuals, each possessed of an unanchored self and all pitted against one another within an amoral structure of pitiless institutions. The secularization of self and community has now reached its apex, and, for the first time, the problem of public morality presents itself in naked profile. What is to be the moral basis of the social order?

Royce had answered this question by retreating into a Pauline communitarianism overlaid with Calvinist virtues; Mead stripped Royce's Pauline–Calvinist conceptions of their religious foundations and put forward the ideal of a co-operative commonwealth guided by the generalized other; Blumer recognized the lingering Protestantisms in Mead's formulation of the relations between mind, self and society, and attempted to ground his community morality in the secular ethics of a public philosophy; Goffman, who recognized the problem of a community without a supererogatory god, posited its solution in the sacralization of the self within a conscience community pledged to the anthropomorphosis of humanity. The time periods in which these conceptions of moral community developed extend from the Civil to the Vietnam Wars.

Royce's central concern in the aftermath of the Civil War was to re-establish the ethical prerequisites for the American community. Struck by the violent character, corrupt politics, and social disorder of American life, he attempted to develop a normative theory of character and social structure that would be consistent with Christian faith (Royce, 1948, pp. 214–96, 393–4). The result was an elaborated version of evolutionism that looked forward to the harmonization of mind, society and God. Royce (1968, pp. 75–98, 229–50; and 1969) regarded the restoration of America as a Christian community as his central philosophical and social concern.[1]

Royce employed a conception of deistic evolution to find the route to a co-operating community. First the 'process of evolution will lead ... from disorderly to a more orderly arrangement', and, he asserted, then this 'philosophy of nature will show ... that, amid all chances [there is] some tendency to orderly cooperation' (Royce, 1969, pp. 732–3). Royce combined his sense of evolution with a conception of the mathematical probabilities for regaining lost community. His probability theory projected equilibrium for any given social arrangement, while his functionalist evolutionary theory proceeded in terms of an ordered series that ultimately would form a single universal community. Within this grand cosmic vision, he preserved a voluntaristic conception of individual action. To Royce (1969, p. 607), social evolution was divinely teleological: 'The world is *also* there to express a perfectly determinate and absolute purpose. Its facts are incidents in a life – yes, in a life of many lives – *a rationally connected social system of beings that embody purposes in deeds.*' Anticipating the idea of the voluntaristic, functionally integrated society, Royce placed the Christian covenant in evolution and inextricably connected the self with all other selves.

For Royce (1916) the Christian community achieves solidarity in what he called a 'philosophy of loyalty'. The noblest expression of the self is expressed in loyalty: the ideal community is a covenant of loyalty, ultimately a covenant of loyal Christian believers. Royce's conception of the community was that of an American Puritan. 'His analysis of living American communities', John G. McDermott (1969, p. 41) points out, 'has much in common with the self-consciousness of the Puritan attempt to forge a new relationship between religious covenant and the police.' Royce saw no contradiction in integrating self, community, religious faith, nation and state.

Royce's national integration of the moral community rested on a philosophy of loyalty, in effect a faith in fidelity itself. His theory of loyalty was dialectical: conflicts between two equally valid group loyalties would be synthesized into a single community loyalty at a higher level. He (1916, pp. 197–248, 349–98) projected the eventual formation of an American communitarian society whose ethos would be both Christian and civil. Royce's 'philosophy of loyalty' appears to be indiscriminant – as, for instance, when he praises equally the loyalty of the unionists and the secessionists in the Civil War to their respective and opposed causes. However, he is employing a dialectical method to resolve antagonisms by pointing to their latent progressive functions. In the Civil War, the pro- and anti-slavery forces 'actually served the one cause of the now united nation. They loyally shed their blood, North and South, that we might be free from their burden of hatred and horror' (Royce, 1916, p. 193). By the same token, Royce (1908a, pp. 224–5) found in the many violent personal, racial, economic and political conflicts that bloodied the first half-century of American frontier history 'a certain idealism, often more or less unconscious', an ultimately progressive 'tension between individualism and loyalty, between shrewd conservation and bold radicalism, which marks this community'. Even racial antipathies – whose instinctive and psychological character Royce felt to be far more the cause of race problems than any alleged inherent inequalities – had positive and progressive functions: ultimately they moved humankind toward a single community (Royce, 1908b, pp. 1–54). Royce provided a social theodicy that converted virtually all human conflicts into harmonies of social value.

The doctrine of Pauline corporatism gave Royce a basis for his own conception of a respiritualized moral community. The parables of Jesus, Royce asserted, revealed the 'two beings to whom Christian love is owed: God and the neighbor'. Paul had introduced a third and more mysterious being, the 'corporate entity'. That 'corporate entity is the Christian community', Royce declared. Paul's religious community had 'a practical concreteness, a clear common sense about it'. Embedded in Paul's restatement of Jesus' commandment to love thy neighbor is a new definition of inclusion in that community: 'For Paul the neighbor has now become a being who is primarily the fellow-member of the Christian community' (Royce, 1968, pp. 93–4). In this conception of the Christian neighbor, Royce discovered an ultimate principle of loyalty as well as the basis for an American national communitarianism founded on altruism and Christian brotherhood.

Secularization of the Self

Royce's conception of a spiritualized community that would reconstitute American society as a Pauline and Puritan brotherhood broke on the shoals of the deepening secularization of American life. George Herbert Mead criticized Royce's ideas because he believed they were at odds with the realities of self, community and society in the United States (Mead, 1964b). He rejected Royce's theory of 'the infinite series involved in self-representation' and the supposedly positive functions of dialectically evolving loyalty as contrary to experience. 'Causes', Mead (1964b, p. 382) observed, 'loyalty to which unites the man to the group, so far from fusing themselves to higher causes till loyalty reaches an ultimate loyalty to loyalty, [as Royce insists], remain particular and seek specific ends in practical conduct, not resolution in an attained harmony of disparate causes of infinity.' Mead treated this aspect of Royce's philosophy as 'part of the escape from the crudity of American life, not an interpretation of it'. Royce's 'individual is American in his attitude, but he calls upon this American to realize himself as an intellectual organization of conflicting ends that is already attained in the absolute self'. Mead (1964b, p. 382) pointed out that 'there is nothing in the relation of the American to his society that provides any mechanism that even by sublimation can accomplish such a realization'.

Having stripped Royce's idealism of its spiritual and metaphysical character, Mead (1964b, p. 382) substituted the secular socio-psychological concept of the generalized other for that of the infinite ideal: 'Royce points out that the individual reaches the self only by a process that implies still another self for its existence and thought'. Mead exorcised the Presbyterian–Pauline Christian synthesis that Royce had constructed and returned the sociology of the self and the community to an inner-worldly pragmatism that had earlier transvalued a de-Catholicized Calvinistic Puritanism. The American did not achieve self-identity from subordination to the community: 'The communities came from him, not he from the community' (Mead 1964b, p. 382). Thus the awesome attitude toward the community that Royce expected would not arise.

Mead located the emergence of community in the processes of communication and interaction, and eliminated eschatology, replacing it with an open-ended history consisting of actions and interactions. For the Infinite Self he substituted the self-reflective self; for Christian values, the generalized other; for the ultimate community of Pauline believers, the penultimate society of interacting selves (Mead, 1964a). In Mead's conception men and women are truly living east of Eden; mind, self and society are without supernatural guidance. Society without God would have to provide its own direction. The ethical, moral and humane bases for modern communities would be given by an undefined generalized other.

Mead's social psychology has retained a conception of the moral individual in a secular world. His conception of the generalized other as each individual's moral arbiter in the secular world allowed him to reformulate the religious ethics of a Puritan community into the civil moralities of a secular society. Mead's conception of civic morality provided the foundation for Herbert Blumer's (1969) symbolic interactionism. However, Blumer had to show how the generalized other might be formed in the face of diverse races, ethnic groups, religious sects, social classes and alternative lifestyles (Lyman, 1984). A multiplicity of apparently irreconcilable definitions of the situation confronted anyone who sought to find community in a single set of values or a co-ordination of sentiments. The pluralization of American society had produced dissent and disharmony: contracultures, communities of limited liability, defensive communities and a host of communities of special and private interest. No common tradition bonded individuals or groups to each other. Heterogeneous beliefs and heterodox sub-cultures posed a fundamental problem: what kind of self, and what kind of community would develop under these conditions?

Blumer (1981, p. 167) observed that, while 'the generalized other is the chief position from which a human participant grasps and understands the social world inside of which he has to develop his conduct', Mead had given 'no aid in tracing how people construct their "generalized others" [nor any] techniques which would enable people ... to improve their ability to take group roles'. Notwithstanding this difficulty, Blumer constructed the moral community on a conception of the generalized other which did not assume a covenanted harmony of interests but rather recognized the necessity for a civil ordering of conflicts.

For Blumer, labor struggles, racial strife and other group conflicts are incidents in the evocation of the generalized other; their resolution is both cause and consequence of its existence. The characteristic feature of the self is self-interaction; however, as he (Blumer, 1981, p. 152) points out, 'self-interaction has the potential of placing an individual in opposition to his associates and to his society'. The problem left unanswered in Blumer's analysis is societal integration: how much opposition can a society tolerate and still evoke a co-operative attitude and a social conscience?

The Situated Self

An unexpected answer to this question is supplied by Erving Goffman. For him, no single relationship or set of relationships can establish a moral code for the individual or for the society as a whole. Every individual has numerous relationships and participates in many groups, each of which demands a display of conformity to its standards (Goffman, 1959). But precisely because each group has or is likely to have different standards, the individual cannot develop a single, universally applicable moral judgement or ethical base line. Goffman's (1959, 1967, 1981) actors do not possess a conscience nor do they recognize a generalized other; rather, they employ the ethics and morality appropriate to a given situation. The individual presents the external signs of acquiescence to the moral standards of a given community, without necessarily having internalized those standards. Each of the relevant communities evaluates the performance and accepts skillful self-presentation as proof that a person does possess the qualities expected. The individual does not develop a unified self with a secure ego and a strong superego. Rather, the society is composed of persons with more or less developed skills of personification. The community is not lost; it achieves its integration through the dramaturgical skills of the actors (Goffman, 1971).

In communities of personification the thrust is away from morally guided interactions and toward resolving dilemmas and problems of strategic interaction. The self is only a presentation, a mask, behind which are other personifications and ultimately only a body. The community is a dramatic construction of interactions in an ever-moving present – without history, without eschatology, a total freedom from which there is no escape and in which there is no God. Thereafter, salvation becomes an inner-worldly burden; the self becomes the only available source for its own sacrament. Individuals, thrown back upon themselves, discover that living up to the requirements of self-sacralization requires a never-ending quest for a self defiled through interaction. A congeries becomes a community when it fulfills this quest. The social compact depends on each human being's willingness to endow the other with the character-istics of a fellow human being. Goffman gives us a new Golden Rule: endow unto others the humanity you wish others to endow unto you. Communities form in obedience to this rule.

The devolution of the moral foundations of community leaves us with one outstanding problem: where can we locate the normative basis for civil society? By granting humanity to one another, each stakes his or her claim to humanity. But, in the process, one is living on behalf of the exaltation of one's own self. A new mundane religion would be required: a sociodicy of self-love based on the presentation of the situated self rather than the contemplation of the morally fixed self. The self-situating actors externalize their love of themselves through endless personifications expressed in the construction and enactment of lifestyles, which become the surrogates of community. Self and lifestyle become warp and woof of the new civil religion that spreads its religious canopy over alternative ways of living. Salvation is achieved without regard to the constraints of the 'generalized other', 'public opinion', or any beliefs in a moral consensus of a community covenant. This civil religion contains its own crisis of legitimation.

No public philosophy can be constructed on a religion of self-love. The moral problem of how to construct the larger civil community remains. People believing in the possibility of community restoration through self-deification have now to confront the future of that illusion.

Society as a Brotherhood of Others

Functional social theory presupposes the organic wholeness of society, conceiving the civil community as its expression and its instrumentality. For both Henry Hughes (1829–62), America's first sociologist, and Talcott Parsons (1903–79), American sociology's pre-eminent functionalist, the organic whole that is said to characterize society arises from the fact of human 'gregation' (to use Hughes's term), but it is organized as a union of federated or interdependent systems (or sub-systems, as Parsons would put it) that act teleologically to accomplish societal ends. Hughes's (1968) division of seven sub-systems embraces no more activity than the smaller set of Parsons's, but Hughes divides it differently into the political, the economic, the hygienic, the philosophic, the esthetic, the ethical and the religious. Whereas for Parsons, the description of the social system is abstract, for Hughes the social system has a definite moral order, and it is directed toward enforcement of a specific moral obligation. Parsons's general system achieves its *telos* in the ever-renewed state of equilibrium, a condition that might contain any organized system of morality; but his universalistic-achievement system, that is, his vision of the moral order of the United States, arises out of an evolution from its Protestant principles (Parsons, 1951, pp. 182–94). In Parsons's imagery, the system is potentially immortal, functioning to perpetuate itself, and achieving an ordered universe by postulation and reinforcement of a common set of core values.

Order as State Coercion
Hughes, in *A Treatise on Sociology*, first published in 1854, defends the

Southern slave system on the basis of a Calvinist doctrine that stresses 'warrantable' callings. To be warrantable, a calling must be ethical and make some contribution to the public good (cf. Weber, 1963). In the face of attacks on the slave system by Northern critics, Southern ideologues were hard pressed to justify the administration of slavery within the framework of Christian doctrine; the role of the slavemaster could not easily be defended as a warrantable calling.[2] Yet, if a link was made between a societal system and its function in fulfilling the work of God, then all members of society – warrantees and warrantors, slaves and masters, men and women – could be thought of as participants in a system of ethically warranted callings. Hughes and the Calvinist Puritans shared the same emphasis in the use of this word, but by his casuistic shift of the warrantable calling from an individual responsibility to a state societal obligation, Hughes was able to ground his theory of the social system in an acceptable religious hermeneutic.

Hughes (1968) sought to organize society around the state enforcement of warrantable callings. At the time he wrote there were in his vision two social systems in the United States, one based on a free market in labor in the North; the other, based on 'warranteeism' and a public obligation to serve in the South. In the North, Hughes complained, there was no public obligation to work or to supervise in the societal interest; there was an absence of caste restrictions on human associations and an indifference toward the regulation, or even the attainment of progress. For Hughes, a liberal, *laissez-faire*, democratic and haphazardly directed society was both immoral and unscientific. 'Warranteeism', on the other hand, found its expression in the institution misnamed slavery. Warranteeism was not slavery, Hughes insisted; it was not 'an obligation to labor for the benefit of the master without the contract or consent of the servant', but rather 'a public obligation of the warrantor and the warrantee, to labor and do other civil duties, for the reciprocal benefit of (1) the State, (2) the Warrantee, and (3) the Warrantor'. 'Property in man', he wrote (1968, p. 167), 'is absurd. Men cannot be owned. In warranteeism, what is owned is the labor-obligation, not the obligee. The obligee is a man.'

With this formulation, Hughes completed the logic of his justification for the slave system. Slave and master are equally necessary to the system, but the participation of the slave, in contrast to slavemaster who is God's steward, is measured by work and industriousness. Hughes secularized the moral foundations of work and gave to the state the duty to enforce them. In his words, 'production is a societary obligation', and it is organized around the distinctions of race and caste. The linking of work ethics to a slave system of production required modifications of Calvinism which Henry Hughes introduced by stratifying the universal obligation to work. His version of the morally ordained producer ethic is, in turn, related to a systemic understanding of political economy linking production, distribution, exchange and consumption. The linkage of these fundamental socio-economic processes is both necessary and possible.

Consumption is the immediate means of subsistence; production, the ultimate. Distribution is intermediate. The perfection of any one of these is the perfection of all. There cannot be perfect production without perfect distribution; nor perfect consumption without both. For distribution and consumption are not ends only of production; they are means of it. (Hughes, 1968, p. 119)

The entire system of production, distribution and consumption depended on incentives and motives. As in the social system envisioned a century later by Parsons, human motivation in Hughes's political economy must be socialized: 'Unless the motives ... are perfect, the product never can be. Men will not work, without they have a good inducement. The better they are induced, the better they produce' (Hughes, 1968, p. 119).

Hughes postulated a social psychology that rested on state administration of fears and desires. He thought that groups who were committed to the system were motivated differently than those not so committed. Planters, intellectuals and skilled labor classes are industrious out of their own self-interests and can be relied upon to do their duty, since in their cases self- and public-interests coincide. Unskilled workers and slaves, on the other hand, could not be counted on to work diligently on their own or society's behalf. Social control of the latter relies on the manipulation of fears and brutal coercion (Hughes, 1968, pp. 89–97, 243–58).[3] Hughes thus combined an authoritarian mechanism for social control with utilitarian motivational theory to construct a comprehensive system of political economy. In doing so, he provided, with a statist theory, the social psychology that linked moral character to social structure. The motivation to work was induced by either force or duty.

The concept of 'duty' in Hughes's work bears a striking similarity to that in Parsons's, with the difference that Parsons's idea of duty is an obligation to the performance of a social role, whereas Hughes's is to the law of God, managed by the state. Choosing to speak for God and to propound a societal system that would administer the ways of God to human beings, Hughes (1968, pp. 291–3) attempted to formulate images of society and of the world that would be consistent with a 'this worldly' Protestant orientation. He invented a species of structural-functionalism, in which the arbiter of the social system was no longer God, but the state.

Order as a Fraternity of Strivers

Social system theory also derived its basic ideas from a synthesis of the social ethics of Francis Greenwood Peabody and the political economy of Frank William Taussig. It was carried forward in Parsons's social psychology of Western capitalism. Thinkers such as Peabody, Taussig and Parsons were concerned to re-establish the brotherhood of man in the face of increasing income, class and ethnic differences, but based their sociology on a crypto-Calvinist utilitarianism. The ethical individual would be an economic achiever and the Christian brotherhood would be a fraternity of strivers.

Peabody propounded an ideology for the redemption of capitalist society and its victims. His sociological theory led him to propose 'the application to organization of the personal power inspired by Jesus Christ' and to demand an ethical stewardship over wealth. As Peabody saw it, the equitable redistribution of wealth would not of itself bring about the moral stance required for those now summoned to prepare the way for the kingdom of God. Because the 'teaching of Jesus permits in no case the sense of absolute ownership', a person *owes* rather than *owns* his or her wealth. And, according to Peabody, Jesus 'asks the whole of one's gains – and the life which lies behind the gains – for the service of the kingdom' (quoted in Hopkins, 1940, p. 212). Peabody's homiletic is similar to that which Henry Hughes had applied. For both Hughes and Peabody there could be no absolute ownership, for a person's wealth is owed and the beneficiary of this obligation is society. Peabody and later sociologists, in contrast to Hughes who had sought to justify a state-ordered economy constructed to support a system of seigniorial socialism, sought to justify a free-market labor economy. By Peabody's day, the inequitable distribution of wealth was so great and so unrelated to personal achievement that the original Puritan theology required a sociodicy that would redefine the mutual obligations of capitalists and workers.

Taussig's economic theory was based on his search for the psycho-social incentive for the 'desire for wealth'. He (Taussig, 1906, pp. 1–3) concluded that this desire is 'not a simple motive, but a very complex one, made up of all sorts of differing passions and interests', including the motivation to work and the desire to achieve. Taussig's orientation was introduced into sociology by Parsons (1936a), who incorporated it into his own theory of motivation. In his essay on motivation, Parsons (1940), who set his own problem as that of finding a theoretical link between personal motives and institutional patterns, posited 'net money advantage' as the decisive variable. The morality of the individual actor of the 'social unit' in whose name the individual acted is thus measurable by the standard of economic achievement. Parsons states:

the fact that concretely economic activities take place in a framework of institutional patterns would imply that, typically, such disinterested elements of motivation play a role in the determination of their course. This is not in the least incompatible with the strict requirements of economic theory, for that requires only that, as between certain alternatives, choice will be made in such a way as to maximize net money advantages to the actor, or to the social unit on behalf of which he acts. (1940 [1965, pp. 58–9])

Connecting Taussig's theory of motivation to his own theory of action, Parsons replaced the Calvinist idea of a calling with the ethic of achievement and provided America's political economy with a system-generated Protestant ethic. Parsons (1978, pp. 167–324) adopted the Protestant orientation as his own, and proclaimed a secular source for salvation through achievement and a sociodicy for the modern world through inevitable progress.

Parsons's sociology contains an eschatology that stands in opposition to that of Marx. Parsons states:

there is a notable resemblance of pattern between what some might call the 'scenario' of Marxism and the basic pattern of Christianity. The Marxist scenario portrays modern man ... as faced with a basically evil social order, although, in the background this ... evil is mitigated by the fact that it has advanced what Marxian theory calls the 'forces of production'. There is, however, in spite of this mitigation, a crying need for radical change, which may even be likened to 'salvation'. This change is to be brought about by a collective act, that of the new working class created by capitalism, the *proletariat*. The act of reorganization or regeneration is thus to come about through revolution, the result of which will be to introduce an ideal state of affairs, in Marxian theory called the state of *communism*. (1979, p. 441)

Conceiving the problem of radical change to be that which leads to salvation, Parsons organized the inner-worldly eschatology of America's social system around the non-revolutionary redemption of the damned. For Parsons as for Hughes the damned are those who have not or will not attain warrantable callings: blacks, women, youths, aliens and deviants. Hughes had resolved their condition by coercing them into obligatory statuses; Parsons by insisting that the system must engender in them the appropriate motivation to achieve. However, Parsons recognized that the major problem troubling the perfectability of his system is its lack of success 'in fulfilling the mission of building the Kingdom of God on Earth', that is, in facilitating the motivation to achieve, the system breeds criminals as well as capitalists, deviants as well as divines. For Parsons the achievement motive is a moral imperative of the system. However the capacity to respond to that moral imperative is constrained by economic conditions and social status.

Hence, in Parsons's (1967, pp. 422–65) 'Keynesian' orientation toward social policy, the state is obliged to aid the dependent, defective and delinquent elements so that they will gain a position from which they can implement the desire to achieve. The social system does not need the state to enforce 'the motivation to achieve', that is a prerequisite to the preservation of the political economy. The motivation is assumed to be uniform throughout the system, and obedience to its demands limits the need for state coercion.

Indeed, Parsons's system resonated with the economic prosperity and large-scale organization of government and business that came to prominence during the New Deal, the Second World War, and the Cold War. His system, grounded on universalism and achievement, was upheld by a stratum of intellectuals and administrators who ostensibly provided purpose and motivation for the strivings of the masses.

Where Hughes's social system is located in its vindication of the ways of God to human beings, the legitimacy of Parsons's system rests on its capacity to re-establish equilibrium in the midst of continuous change (Lipset, 1979; Lyman, 1975). Hughes's system was undone by the Civil War; Parsons's by the collapse of America's moral consensus and political economy during the 1960s and 1970s. Those sociologists who had not presupposed the moral foundations of society confronted once more the fundamental problem of relating state, ethics and public morality. The social system, lacking consensual foundation and a universal moral order, has become a cockpit of competing faiths, doctrines and eschatologies.

Conclusion

The two major traditions of sociological thought in America have contained a gradual dissolution of any well-reasoned discourse about the importance of and circumstances surrounding public morality. On the one hand, public morality has been reduced to an egoistical situated ethics in the pragmatist tradition. Actors are seen as adopting, without critical reflection, standards associated with the various persona they assume. On the other hand, public morality has become a postulated brotherhood in the functionalist tradition, wherein the achievement motivation is adopted as a universal moral imperative. From either tradition, there now appears to be no way to begin a fresh consideration of today's social issues and the moral dilemmas they pose. Importantly, both theoretical stalemates result from similar origins in Protestant religion, suggesting that the project of sociological theory, at least in the United States, had an inherent limitation from the start. According to Mannheim (1943, p. 18), Cooley described this limitation as 'the paradox of Christianity [in] that it tried to apply the virtues of a society based upon neighbourly relationships to the world at large'.

The current stalemate in American sociological theory is alarming given that American society has become continental in scope but not unified by common values capable of forming a national philosophy. To the degree that there is integration, it is accomplished by means of the mass media and electronic interaction. The resulting sense of community is premised upon the closeness of media-projected intimacy, a faith that the staged front is the same as the backstage. Unresolved contradictions and moral dilemmas are sublimated by means of a constantly shifting social reality that is constructed by managers of the new technologies. The spirit of small-town values supplies but one of the ethics of electronically integrated society. Others are provided by images of phantasmagoric other-worlds, exotic and idiosyncratic lifestyles, athletic supermen and women, visions of an America reborn through the electronic church, and celebrations of violence, sex and pornography. The society so integrated abjures the quest for an ethically-grounded public morality, acquiescing to the public relations of front-stage imagery as if that is all there can be.

Notes

This essay explores themes developed in Vidich and Lyman, 1985.

1   The basic image of society projected by Royce had deep theological roots, extending back to Puritan doctrine. Perkins (d. 1602), for instance, cast into military terms his search for a social order amid what he conceived to be the moral chaos of the sixteenth century. Order was a duty imposed by God, he asserted; disorder, anarchy and social unrest were products of Satanic subversion. Order found its expression in each person's obedience to his or her calling. Each calling, in turn, imposed separate and specific duties. Precisely because a calling depended on distinctive talents that were themselves gifts from God, this inner-worldly theology justified a hierarchical social order. The *unequal* social and worldly forms of authority were just, for, as Perkins put it, 'God hath appointed, that in every society one person should be above or under another; not making all equal, as though the bodies should be all head and nothing else; cf. Morgan, 1965, pp. 37–51).

2   For a good example of a then contemporary attempt to vindicate slavery within the canons of Christianity, see Thornton Stringfellow, 'A brief examination of scripture testimony on the institution of slavery', Richmond *Religious Herald*, 25 February 1841, reprinted in Faust, 1981, pp. 136–67.

3   For Hughes's specific proposals of modes of coercion and debrutalization see Ronald T. Takaki, 1971, pp. 84–5.

PART III

TRADITIONS IN DISSOLUTION

4

Sociological Theory and Politics

Peter Lassman

Politics has always presented a special problem for sociological theorists. The classical theorists, from Saint-Simon and Comte to Parsons, wanted to create a body of theory, scientific in form, that would transcend the existing tradition of political thought and which would refuse to grant the realm of the political any special status.

This desire to establish an autonomous body of sociological theory has taken various forms in its long history. The classical theorists assumed both the existence of and the necessity for a clear demarcation between a progressively scientific sociology and a declining tradition of political thought, and this has been a fundamental theme in modern sociology as well. In its most extreme manifestations the desire to eliminate political controversy both from social life and from theoretical reflection upon social life has taken the form of an argument that a mature social science will eradicate the perpetual disagreements that characterize modern political life. This attitude has been expressed very clearly by Roberto Unger.

> Much of social science has been built as a citadel against metaphysics and politics. Faithful to the outlook produced by the modern revolt against ancient philosophy, the classic social theorists were anxious to free themselves first from the illusions of metaphysics, then from the seeming arbitrariness of political judgments. They wanted to create a body of objective knowledge of society that would not be at the mercy of metaphysical speculation or political controversy, and, up to a point, they succeeded. (Unger, 1976, pp. 266–7)

The history of the quest for autonomy from politics is paralleled by another history – the history of the recognition of the inadequacy of the attempt. One line of development in this second history has attended to the failure to produce anything that even remotely resembles a scientific

sociology. Another has proceeded from the consideration that even if we
do produce such a science, it will not be, and cannot be, politically neutral.
Critics in this tradition have substantiated this claim in various ways by:
making it clear that sociological theories exist within a politically bounded
space; showing that the theories were either explicitly to have political
consequences, or implicitly to be absorbed into contemporary political
debates; noticing that the underlying concerns of these theorists were
often political in nature; and arguing that the very attempt to construct, or
to propose the construction of, a social science cannot avoid having a
political dimension.

Max Weber's reported assertion that 'all ultimate questions without
exception are touched by political events, even if the latter appear to be
superficial' (Mayer, 1956, p. 15), reflects this line of critique; the
character of politics is itself such that it can, at least, coexist uneasily with
the project of constructing a social science (Habermas, 1974; Wolin,
1981).

The Shadow of Politics

The recurrence of supposedly eliminated political themes is recognized,
often ambivalently and ambiguously, in many surveys of modern theory.
Persistence of 'meta-theory' has continued to be a source of embarrass-
ment or, at least, a puzzle to all those who have clung to the belief in the
project of a scientific sociology. A central feature of meta-theoretical
analysis of the major traditions of sociological theory has been the
somewhat reluctant admission that the boundary between a body of pre-
scientific social theory and an allegedly scientific sociological theory is
very difficult to draw.

A visible sign of this difficulty is the divergence between the
increasingly technical and methodological refinement of 'empirical'
sociology and a generally non-cumulative body of social theory. There
exists very little in the way of genuine theoretical and conceptual
continuity between these two projects. Aron has suggested that this
dualistic development is most marked when we recognize that social
theory can be characterized as consisting of a collection of doctrines. 'A
doctrine', he says,

> is more than or different from a theory. The word doctrine suggests a
> complex body of judgements of fact and judgements of value, a social
> philosophy as well as a system of concepts or of general propositions.
> (Aron, 1968, p. v)

Considered as doctrines, the concerns of sociology have familiar affinities.
Dahrendorf points out that the themes of sociological theory, 'power,

resistance, conflict, historical change, openness, freedom, uncertainty' are not shared.

Inevitably, the sociological perspective made up by such notions is a political and philosophical perspective as well. It is the perspective of a modern liberalism: averse to Utopia in sociological theory as in political practice (and in that sense neither 'conservative' nor 'radical'), always looking for ways to guarantee individual liberty in a world of constraints, confident in the ability of the right social and political institutions to provide the possibility of free human development, and skeptical of all theories and approaches in social science that ignore or reflect the question of what they have to contribute to bringing about a society in which men may be free. (Dahrendorf, 1968, pp. viii-ix)

Dahrendorf's attitude to this affinity between the two types of theory is ambivalent. He concedes that the verifiable sociological theories promised by 'theories of society' are, at present, non-existent – and that it is the duty of the sociologist to move from a fascination with theories of society (what Aron calls 'doctrines'), to the development of specific sociological theories.

Yet major areas of sociological inquiry are permeated by seemingly insoluble meta-theoretical disputes, and a vague unease seems to occur whenever the state of entire sociological theory is discussed. The continual pleas for reconstruction seem to be an indication of this state of affairs. One recent discussion was 'written in the belief that there is a widespread feeling among sociologists that contemporary social theory stands in need of a radical revision' (Giddens, 1971, p. vii). Yet the dead hand of the classical theorists continues to be the visible hand: another survey sees the classics as the producers of 'images of society' that make a substantial contribution to many of the problems that are, or should be, 'major theoretical issues in today's sociology' (Poggi, 1972, p. xi). These themes, the persistent relevance of the classics, and the continued dissatisfaction with contemporary theory, are repeated throughout the literature that advocates the reconstruction of sociological theory.

An interesting, and in many ways symptomatic, attempt to break away from this impasse has been put forward by Giddens. Recognizing the existence of a 'Babel of theoretical voices', he outlines three typical reactions: despair or disillusionment coupled with an attitude that ignores theory and gets on with social research; a reversion to dogmatism, asserting the superiority of one preferred theory over all others with the minimum of argument; and lastly a rejoicing at the diversity of perspectives and theories. Despite the apparently radical nature of this diagnosis of contemporary theoretical debates, Giddens ultimately follows a path which parallels earlier discussions of theory.

At first he is attracted to an argument of pluralism and diversity. This view has much to recommend it, he says.

For it can plausibly be argued that chronic debates and persistent dissension about how the study of human conduct is to be approached express something about the very nature of human social conduct itself; *that deeply established disagreements about the nature of human behaviour are integral to human behaviour as such, and thus necessarily intrude into the heart of the discourse of philosophy and social theory.* (Giddens, 1979, p. 239; my emphasis)

Giddens withdraws from the implications of this important insight. His own response follows a long history of attempts to construct an apparently apolitical system of theory; the only way forward, we are told is to attempt a 'systematic reconstruction' of social theory. As Giddens notes, any such proposed reconstruction could simply substitute a new orthodoxy for an old one, and this forces him back to considering problems of the history of sociology. One of the central issues facing attempts to reconstruct sociological theory is the undermining of the prevailing 'self-interpretation of its origins' held by mainstream sociologists, namely that sociology is still considered to be a 'young science' developing along a path similar to that traversed by the natural sciences. Another issue likely to be encountered is the belief that there was a radical break in the emergence of social science from pre-existing traditions of social and political philosophy.

The latter problem, of political roots anchoring an apolitical social science, has been discussed by Bottomore. He summarizes the way in which, with some possible exceptions, the territory of modern sociological theory has been defined and has shifted in relation to political debates and conflicts, traditional features of social theory. A distinctively modern element, Bottomore claims, is that social theory redefines the territory of modern politics because 'social theories themselves came to be seen in quite a new way, as a necessary foundation for political doctrines' (Bottomore, 1983, p. 41). This triumph of social theory follows the argument that the history of social theories must be seen as more than just a history of ideologies. Bottomore concedes that a theorist's work may be shaped by a mixture of influences derived from the political and cultural debates of his own time and place. But he holds that the activity of theorizing possesses its own autonomous logic that allows the finished theoretical product to be evaluated in purely scientific terms which pay no particular attention to that originating context. This account parallels the standard one propounded by Parsons and Merton and recently revived by Alexander (Alexander, 1982; Merton, 1957; Parsons, 1937).

This traditional narrative of sociological theory usually takes for granted that the relationship between a social theorist's political beliefs and his scientific achievements is a one-way street. Yet most of the classical sociological theorists were engaged in political commentary, and it is often in their political commentary that we find a clear expression of their social theory. Marx's 18th *Brumaire* or Weber's 'Parliament and government in a reconstructed Germany' (1978) cannot be neatly classified as either 'political opinion' or as 'social science' nor in terms of a contrast between science and ideology. This suggests that in writing commentary the political significance of a social theory is revealed, and hence it is a mistake to think that there is some radical break between commentary and theory. As Sheldon Wolin says, 'the theorist-turned-commentator has not shed his theoretical view. Rather, he has used the theory to inform his commentary and he has made of commentary an intimation of his theory' (Wolin, 1980, p. 191).

The work of Talcott Parsons, in which we see evidence of tensions and ambiguities central to, and indeed constitutive of, what has become known as the sociological tradition, exhibits this same relation between commentary and theory. Parsons, perhaps more than any other recent theorist, saw clearly what claims must be made in order to argue for the possibility and the necessity of a general social science. Most of his many critics did not see what was theoretically distinctive about his work and, consequently, failed to see that they too shared many of his own presuppositions. Despite the fact that Parsons's own starting point is the 'problem of order' defined in Hobbesian terms, the direction of the argument exemplified in his *The Structure of Social Action* is to direct sociological theory away from questions of politics. Nevertheless, the central argument that sociology must be clearly defined as being distinct from politics and economics, as 'the science which attempts to develop an analytical theory of social action systems in so far as these systems can be understood in terms of the property of common-value integration' (Parsons, 1937, p. 768), is itself closely tied to an implicit political purpose. On the penultimate page of *The Structure of Social Action* he defends his theoretical project in what are, in effect, political terms. He warns against the 'strong current of pessimism', especially among sociologists, which sees all theory as being ultimately arbitrary and subjective, because the consequences of this attitude are to produce either a hyper-empiricism or, more dangerously, an attitude of 'irrationalism' (Parsons, 1937, p. 774).

The attempt to construct a social science in this form will always face the problem of demonstrating the superiority of one theory over its rivals in a competition to establish a shared vocabulary by which a given subject matter can be characterized. Indeed, Parsons had to argue, as did Marx and

Durkheim before him, that his own science transcends the ideologies of others. He uses the case of Weber to demonstrate the way in which a true social science can emerge free from ideological contamination. He argues that it is impossible to classify Weber politically as a liberal, a conservative, or a socialist because his thought points to a 'fourth position' in terms of which these political ideologies have lost their meaning. In other words, Parsons enlists Weber as an advocate of the famous 'end of ideology' thesis. Just as the 'end of ideology' is proclaimed, however, an old sociological dream reappears.

> Our science may well be destined to play a major role, not only in its primary task of understanding the social and cultural world we live in as object of its investigations but, in ways which cannot be foreseen, in actually shaping that world. (Parsons, 1971, p. 50)

This dream is the dream of a 'rational politics' that will emerge on the basis of a firm foundation of scientific sociological knowledge.

A Tradition of Paradox

The paradox within the mainstream sociological tradition is that it attempts to make two divergent claims. On the one hand it is claiming to construct, now or in a not too distant future, a genuine social science that will apply to all social phenomena, including political phenomena. On the other hand a fundamental motive and desired outcome for this is the creation of a rational political order. Parsons's general theory is simply one of the more recent attempts to do this, but it seems that from Comte to Habermas's more recent writings, there has been a continuous series of attempts to tame the political. That this is itself a political activity only deepens the problem (Habermas, 1974).

If the tradition of sociological thought is examined closely in these terms, we find that all attempts to construct a general theory reach their limits with an attempt to include the political realm. Sociological theory in its classical form attempted to establish a scientific self-understanding that conceals a political and moral discourse. Distinctions between 'ideology' and 'science', as well as schemes of social and moral evolution which relegated opposed schemes to the past, provided the appearance of a secure foundation for claims to an epistemologically privileged position. The development of the concept of 'ideology' illustrates the limits of this attempt. The critical use of the concept of 'ideology' has always foundered on the problem of establishing a non-ambiguous distinction between the ideological and the non-ideological that would be neither self-refuting nor dogmatic.

The difficulties of today's paradox have deep roots in the bodies of nineteenth- and twentieth-century social and political thought, appropriated to form the concept of the 'sociological tradition'. Classical theorists, and especially those influenced by Hegel and Marx, realized an essential characteristic of modernity; for the first time methodologically reflective social theorists understand that their own theories make a significant contribution towards the *constitution* of those same social phenomena they seek to interpret and explain. The point holds for political and social thought generally.

A political theory, and the theory of knowledge attached to it, are part of the consciousness, and of the self-conscious attitudes, which they also interpret. This interplay between theory and fact is generally missed by positivists, both old and new, and by liberal theorists. A causal relation between belief in a specific theory of social change, and of the consciousness that the social change requires, they will of course acknowledge; but a more intimate reflexive relation, in which theory is part of the state of consciousness which it interprets, is not recognised. Under modern conditions of literacy, a theory can rapidly enter into the identifications, the loyalties and the sense of affliction and alienation, which it purports to describe, and by which it was to some degree inspired. (Hampshire, 1973, p. 75)

The sociologist is thus also a social agent and the general propositions that he makes concerning social life must refer to his own conduct as well as to that of others.

Reflexive application need not, in itself, mean that a social science is impossible to construct, but it does set up a barrier that has to be overcome. When social theorists attempt to discuss the political life of a society, or the political implication and consequences of social life in a way that they claim is itself free from political implications, they are faced with some fundamental problems. The social theorist, in putting forward general theories of society or attempting to construct explanations of aspects of social life, is necessarily involved in a *competition* with the theories and explanations offered by the agents in question themselves and with the theories and explanations offered by other social theorists – what Giddens calls the 'double hermeneutic' of sociological concepts (Giddens, 1979). The 'double hermeneutic' has a political dimension; the sociologist is not suspended neutrally over the conflict of interpretations that characterizes modern societies. Because he claims a kind of legitimacy for his interpretations, he cannot ignore the politics of interpretation. The demands of the arena in which legitimacy is established include a 'limitation to pure interpretation', 'set by the oppositional mode of contemporary politics' (Connolly, 1981, p. 37).

One escape from this problem is to put forward a form of evolutionary account in terms of which the evolution of social science is firmly grounded in the evolution of society itself. Social science, in this account, becomes the self-consciousness of society. As Parsons puts it, the social sciences are increasingly insulated from ideological distortion as social science itself becomes institutionalized within its own sub-system of 'cognitive rationality'. Parsons thus envisions an escape from the paradoxes of reflexivity at the level of different institutional sub-systems committed to distinctive cognitive aims. But when Parsons's theory is applied to specific topics, such as the American university system, it is obvious that the account given is not politically neutral at all. To some it 'is a muddle which conceals a nightmare' (Wolin, 1974, p. 40).

The Characterization of Politics

The difficulties surrounding this tradition of paradox have sometimes been approached directly by a sociological inquiry into the character of political discourse. Such an inquiry is pursued in a provocative way by Mannheim in his essay 'The prospects of scientific politics'. Since this has typically been perceived as a flawed but important contribution to a sub-discipline called 'the sociology of knowledge', it is not surprising that its central political themes have been neglected. Mannheim addresses the question, what do we mean by politics?

Political conduct, however, is concerned with the state and society insofar as they are still in the process of becoming. Political conduct is confronted with a process in which every moment creates a unique situation and seeks to disentangle out of this everflowing stream of forces something of enduring character. The question then is: 'Is there a science of this becoming, a science of creative activity?' (Mannheim, 1936, p. 100)

An overlooked but central feature of political life is its unpredictability. It possesses an innovative character that cannot be subsumed under law-like generalizations (MacIntyre, 1972). One reason for this is that the outcome of political disputes cannot be predicted. As Marx stated:

A distinction should always be made between the material transformation of the economic conditions of production, which can be determined with the precision of natural science, and the legal, political, religious, aesthetic, or philosophic – in short, ideological forms in which men become conscious of this conflict and fight it out. (Marx, 1977, pp. 389–90)

Mannheim makes an analogous point. He states clearly that true political understanding can never attain the form of a closed theoretical system which can be radically separated from its own subject matter. Political thought is not pure theory. It cannot become a genuine system of concepts, theories or laws that are remote from practical activity and the understanding of particular events and phenomena. Yet Mannheim's own discussion of this moves, in a way that is symptomatic of much social theory, in two opposed directions. An account of political judgement as a practice in which the theorist reflects upon particular ideologies operating within a specific context is constrained by a counter attempt to terminate this reflection in the form of a synthesizing social science, characterized in terms either of the role of the intellectuals or of the rationality of social planning.

One of the basic assumptions that weakens Mannheim's project is the belief that the realm of the political is an essentially irrational one. Mannheim identifies the social with rationality, or the process of rationalization, and the political with an uncontrolled, irrational sphere. The trend of social development is to reduce the scope of the irrational. The result is that, despite a recognition of the character of political understanding, Mannheim is more concerned to move in a direction that corresponds with the mainstream of *sociological* thought, and devalues and ignores the specific character of *politics*. The tendency to regard the political as an inherently irrational sphere is a theme that runs throughout the history of sociology. In the case of Max Weber the characterization of an unending conflict of values is well known. However, the opposition between social rationalization and an uncontrollable cultural irrationality leads, at times in Weber's social thought, to an assertion of the 'illusion of politics' (Brener, 1982; Furet, 1981). Weber's emphasis upon an essentially irrational political sphere of conflicting ultimate values, contrasted with the rationality of science, creates the conditions for the political to acquire a 'mythical' form. His personal despair with the contemporary political situation had an affinity with his vision of the relation in which an advocacy of political neutrality in social science was combined with an exaggerated picture of the political domain as an arena in which only unbounded sovereign subjects, either as political leaders or as great nation-states, could impose some sort of order through the exercise of political will.

The Irreducibility of the Political

Despite the errors which both Weber and Mannheim created by overloading the dichotomy between the rationality of social organization and the irrationality of politics, they recognize that the central problems to social theory are political in nature and that any attempt at constructing a general sociological theory cannot fail to imply the exercise of political judgement and understanding. To build on this recognition would lead us to see that the theorist is not involved in a struggle between science and ideology, but in a mediation between detached reflection and responsible involvement, not merely in the business of subsuming particular instances under general laws, but in *judging* the relevance of particulars for general interpretations. This form of understanding is not captured by the normal textbook accounts of prescriptive methodology, nor can it be formalized into a set of rules for theory construction (Beiner, 1983).

As Weber often pointed out, the development of social science is always shaped by practical questions (Weber, 1949, p. 61). But as a consequence it cannot avoid ethical and political questions. At the centre of Weber's methodological essays there is even the question: what is good for man and, by implication, what is the good society? (Bellah, 1983; Weber, 1949, p. 27). To be sure, classical sociological theorists tended, on the whole, to push to the margins of their thought any recognition of the dualism contained in the concept of politics. They discussed the operation of power and created a sub-discipline of political sociology, but they did not, and perhaps could not, make explicit the other side of the concept that refers not to phenomena of rule and power but to the endless process of political argument and the open-ended and indeterminate nature of political practice (Gallie, 1973). To have done so would have raised the question of the political dimension of their own social theories in a way that would have been seriously threatening to the whole project of a social science.

The inability to formulate a coherent political theory 'may well be the meaning of social science' (Wolin, 1981, p. 405). But even when the claim to scientific status is either abandoned or seriously modified this does not necessarily imply the end of all attempts to construct general social theories, which seem inevitably to reduce the political, in both senses, to what are claimed to be more fundamental social realities (Habermas, 1983a). Modern social science, in this account, has been just one fairly coherent moment in a longer history of attempts to cope with a very uncomfortable fact.

5

Morality, Self and Society: the Loss and Recapture of the Moral Self

Ellsworth R. Fuhrman

> I have tried to show that in [Immanuel Kant's] alleged dictates of reason the emotional background is transparent throughout. And if I have succeeded in such an attempt in the case of the greatest of all moral rationalists, I flatter myself with the belief that I have in no small measure, given additional strength to the main contention of this book: that the moral consciousness is ultimately based on emotions, that the moral judgement lacks objective validity, that the moral values are not absolute but relative to the emotions they express. (Westermarck, 1970, p. 289)

Since the First World War, few social scientists have continued explicitly to embrace the Enlightenment belief that a science of society will improve the moral fiber of individuals and/or societies. Instead, many sociologists might argue today that the rational moralism of the Enlightenment project was doomed to fail, and that its passing opened the way for a 'pure' science of society, one without a concern for political practice. Such a cursory dismissal of the broader aims of the Enlightenment project overlooks the possibility of retaining certain of the moral ambitions of the project while discarding those which have been rendered irrelevant by the circumstances of 'advanced' societies dominated by multinational corporations. We might begin to assess the Enlightenment project by looking at possible explanations for its 'failure'.

Numerous and varied accounts have been offered for the failure of the Englightenment project, although they can be parsimoniously divided into two groups. *External* accounts have shown that some feature of the larger society (for example, the inherently conservative nature of bureaucracy, state socialism or monopoly capitalism) has blocked the practical fulfillment of the Enlightenment project. *Internal* accounts have identified contradictory themes in Enlightenment thought itself. This essay pursues an internal assessment of the Enlightenment project as it was worked out in sociological thought. However, the intent is not to destroy but to reinvigorate the Enlightenment project and restore its original promise – a moral/political discourse anchored in reason and intended to guide political practice for advancing human relations.

Inconsistent Themes

'Man is born free, and yet is everywhere in chains' (Rousseau, 1947, p. 5). Rousseau's famous statement neatly locates two inconsistent themes in Enlightenment thought. On the one hand, each individual is born with a particular human nature which enables him or her to be self-directed. Yet society everywhere encircles individuals, controlling the range of individual activities and potentialities. The legacy of these inconsistent themes was a problem of man in society, and solutions to the problem characteristically took the form of identifying the 'master principle' governing the relations of the two. On one side of these discussions was the theme of a critical standard for evaluating modern institutions which stifled human development; the secret to developing society and thereby individuals was finding the appropriate social structure which enabled people to express their potentiality. The other side of the discussion generally avoided the idea that human nature was shaped by society; human nature was thought to be biologically and/or physiologically endowed with fixed qualities, which in turn shaped the organization of society.

Historical irony has prevailed and the 'master principle' solutions themselves are partially to blame for the waning of Enlightenment concerns. The post-Enlightenment conceptions of human nature and society did not have the universality and a historicity they pretended, a characteristic shared with Sophist conceptions of 'natural man'. As MacIntyre argues:

> The factual point is, then, that the so-called natural man is merely a man from another and earlier culture. The conceptual point is that this is no accident. For the character of pre-social man is described in terms of certain traits which he possesses; selfishness, aggressiveness, and the like. But these traits, or rather words which name and characterize them and enabled them to be socially recognized traits, belong to a vocabulary which presupposes an established web of social and moral relationships. Words like *selfish*, *unselfish*, *aggressive*, *mild*, and the like are defined in terms of established norms of behavior. (MacIntyre, 1980, pp. 17–18)

The inconsistent themes of Enlightenment thought were often publicly expressed in separate moral and conflicting political agendas. The broader aims of the Enlightenment project have disappeared, but these inconsistent themes remained in sociological discourse. The justification for each now rests on a foundation distinguished by a conception of science as value-neutral. In effect, sociological discourse has become publicly more amoral. In the rest of this essay, I discuss the increasingly amoral discourse of sociology as it relates to the continuation of the inconsistent themes reflected in more recent conceptions of self and society. In addition, I suggest an alternative vision of self and society that would overcome the inconsistency as well as restore the promise of the Enlightenment project.[1]

The Disappearance of the Moral Self into Human Nature

Great importance in accounts of social theory is often and quite correctly attributed to the Enlightenment and counter-Enlightenment treatments of human nature (Berlin, 1982; Cassirer, 1951, 1970; Gay, 1963, 1977; Mannheim, 1971), and sociologists have made extensive use of them (Gouldner, 1973; Nisbet, 1968) in the course of developing their own style of thought. One line of theorizing attempted to work out the relationship between human nature and society by stabilizing human nature, endowing it with 'natural passions' (Hobbes, 1969, p. 115). Adam Smith (1967), for example, noted that the division of labor 'from which so many advantages are derived' is but a product 'of a certain propensity in human nature'.

More recently, some theorists have refined the analysis of exchange processes (Blau, 1964; Homans, 1961) but with little appreciable advancement on Smith's original argument about the division of labor. In exchange theory, an amoral actor makes choices on a 'rational' basis (often with incomplete information) to maximize rewards. Rewards for the latter-day theorists are construed very broadly to include material and symbolic elements. However, in these formulations the actor has no sense of justice or equity except in so far as these can be related to an inherent reward structure. Blau (1964, p. 18) notes that 'moral standards clearly do guide and refrain human conduct. Within the rather broad limits those norms impose on social relations, however, *human beings tend to be governed in their associations with one another by the desire to obtain social rewards* of various sorts and the resulting exchanges of benefits shape the structure of social relations' (my emphasis).

In addition to an innate propensity for trucking and bartering, other attempts were made to reduce the moral self to a basic human nature. A motley group of 'natural', physiological, biological and psychological properties appeared in the writing of early American sociologists (Fuhrman, 1980). These efforts at endowing human nature with particular ahistorical characteristics often functioned to perpetuate various political ideologies (MacPherson, 1972; Schwendinger and Schwendinger, 1974). Indeed, the sociological classics, when they address the fundamental nature of human beings, inevitably contain implications for what human beings and their societies ought to be.

The Disappearance of the Moral Self into Society

In contrast to the disappearance of the moral self into the drives, instincts or forces of a human nature physiologically or biologically endowed, an inconsistent theme was also at work which drove the moral self into the fabric of social circumstances. Here the moral self disappeared into a master principle of society encircling individuals, such as division of labor, relations of production, or bureaucracy. The self in this instance became a victim of social conditions. As a victim the self was linked with a theoretical strategy which: (1) tended to associate changes in one segment of society (e.g. the economy) with uniform changes throughout society; or (2) acted as if all the ruptures and disjunctures of modern society were spatial in nature, reducing the self to a bearer of social structure. The political impetus behind either approach denies the self any morality while opening the avenue to therapeutically managed societies containing ahistorical, anonymous and plastic individuals.

The reduction of the moral self into society can perhaps best be captured by briefly examining different answers to the question, how is social order possible? There have been at least three major responses: (1) tradition, habit and custom; (2) norms, values; and (3) coercion, exploitation.[2] These answers to the question of social order, although they can be differentiated along an ideological continuum from right to left, have this in common: they remove the moral actor from the center stage of social life and continue the quest for a master principle.

William Graham Sumner (1840–1910) expended a great deal of energy examining and analyzing tradition through the folkways and mores of social life. In Sumner's view the folkways and mores were products of evolutionary experience, and 'World philosophy, life policy, rights and morality are all products of the folkways' (Sumner, 1940, p. 29). 'Custom is a social fact which dominates our lives and to which we cannot help in appealing. Custom is by its nature a floating and undefined conception, and is accepted as a sort of pervasive and irreducible feature of life … all of society's forms and institutions are found, when reduced to lowest evolutionary terms, in custom' (Sumner and Keller, 1927, pp. 30–31). This view of the foundation of social order suggests that, in the evolution of the species, institutions (for example, private property, marriage) arose as *solutions* to the concrete problems of nature and society. The central characteristic of their evolution was the non-intentional nature of their development. They were and are unconscious responses which appear to work, that is, allow individuals to survive and adapt to changing circumstances. In effect, this formulation suggests that habit and tradition constitute the hidden and largest part of our social life. Like an iceberg, tradition overwhelms the majority of life and consciousness, and moral decision-making is only the tip, the non-salient part of daily actions. The moral actor is subsumed by tradition and habit.

Another consensual view of society argues that common norms and values, not tradition, are the bases of social order. Though there has been little agreement about the range and emotional attachment to values, or the norms derived from them, the theory of 'normative integration' seems to leave room for a moral 'voluntaristic' decision-making actor. Actors work out their lives within the context of a symbolic environment (Parsons, 1937), but they are not moral actors making political choices and compromises between opposing sets of values emanating from different sectors of society. The options, as well as the methods by which to select from them, are limited (cf. Bourricaud, 1981). Not even deviation from the prevailing values (Merton, 1938) is described in moral concepts but rather in the terms of functional adaption. This leaves no theoretical space for the moral actor; functional men cannot revolt against injustice, for prejudice is not a social science category. Rebellion is evaluated for its functional significance rather than for the force of its moral claims (Moore, 1973, 1978). These theories, ironically, are presented as value-free.

Another theoretical strategy for exploring the bases of social order depends on the notion that coercion and exploitation order the social universe. Here the actor is reduced to fear and trembling still without a moral self. The basis for his/her actions may be fear of the chaos that would ensue without a strong ruler, a matter of accepting domination by another class, manipulation by political elites, and so on. A great deal of social science literature which is not explicitly concerned with the bases of social order takes for granted that social actors are not primarily exchange oriented or normative but rather fearful creatures. People are assumed to act in certain ways because they fear losing their jobs, losing status, or fear political consequences. But actors often rise above their fears and refuse to be coerced or exploited, and they are willing to live with the consequences of their actions because of a moral commitment. Sociologists, arriving on the scene at a later date, reduce this moral motivation to consideration of the external forces which determine the actors' behavior.

All of these responses to the question of social order are reductive and in each the morality of the self disappears. Selves have no moral/political[3] interests independent of society, and people who attempt to actualize an independent self often receive the sociological label 'deviant'. Here again the values of sociologists are hidden from view by an amoral sociological discourse. The master principles describe a theoretical world of perfect integration between actors and their societies, a world which scarcely resembles modern societies. Such discourses may have limited theoretical utility within modern societies. There are practical implications of this as well, for the disappearance of the moral self has generally been associated with the rise of an equally sterile view of social reform.

Science, Social Reform and the Amoral Self

Although many of the early sociologists wanted to make sociology scientific, and therefore free of moral exhortation, they were never particularly successful. The 'scientific' conceptions of human nature and society were mere reifications. Thus attempts to make sociology scientific led to the development of the ideological elitism inherent in the claim to 'scientific' expertise (Wardell and Fuhrman, 1981). If human activity was physiologically or sociologically inclined towards certain kinds of behavior, only those people who had knowledge of these inclinations, namely sociologists, could properly direct the course of events (Durkheim, 1938). Others, less informed than sociologists, ought to listen to and heed their advice. This was a mild form of elitism; some forms were more virulent. E. A. Ross issued a call to be Machiavellian.

> In the taming of men there must be coil after coil to entangle the unruly ones. Manquellers must use snares as well as leading string, will-o-wisps as well as lanterns. The truth by all means if it will promote obedience, but in any case, obedience. (Ross, 1914, p. 304)

For the most part, prior to the First World War, the sociological heirs to the Enlightenment expressed an underlying optimism about what a science of society could accomplish. Generally, however, sociologists believed that 'good' and 'progressive' social reform could be achieved only if the methods and procedures of science were followed. The therapeutic motive (Rieff, 1966) meant that much of early sociology was linked with reform and reform movements. Often enough, this linkage varied from one country to another.

As sociology grew, the link between sociological discourse and reform became less obvious for those interested in reform, who increasingly saw sociology as irrelevant, and was broken by sociologists adamantly opposed to the link in the first place. The effect of these trends was to remove morality further from conceptions of human nature. Dennis Wrong (1961) castigated Parsons for an 'oversocialized' view of human nature, and offered a sterile individual full of hidden desires in return. Erving Goffman's (1959) presentation of the self reveals a nameless individual behind an amoral, apolitical mask whose main purpose is to save face. The removal of the notion that selves are moral/political decision-makers was now complete. At the same time as the realm of the moral was being removed from human nature by sociologists of the 1950s, 1960s and 1970s, it was also being removed from the conception of society. The introduction of social systems theory, and especially Bell's (1976) treatment of a post-industrial society, paralleled the rejection of the link between science and social reform. Social reform, if it was discussed, appeared in a calculus of instrumental terms (Habermas, 1970).

The linkage between sociological discourse, morality and social reform is complicated because of the various ways it has been historically worked out. Nevertheless, in spite of the attempts to rid moral and political concerns from sociological theory, a moral discourse remains buried within the project because it: expresses an ethical telos, has underlying value interests, possesses a discourse impossible to separate from everyday moral discourse; and has moral effects in terms of social reform.

Toward a Reinvigoration of Moral Discourse

To restore the moral self to a central place in sociological thinking necessitates a different vision of the self–society relationship than the one offered by the tradition of sociological theory, including its Marxist component. Modern societies do not exhibit the coherence that some social theorists would like to see (Bell, 1976). Rather, modern societies are non-synchronous; they are 'multilayered' in time and space. Often spatial differences (for example, class divisions) are mediated, complemented, and contradicted by temporal horizons.

For example, traditional distinctions in the analysis of societies prove to be ineffective in analyzing multinational corporations. There is evidence to suggest that the cultural hegemony often enjoyed by individual nation-states is being shattered by the multinational corporation (Horowitz, 1974). The multinationals, in contrast to the firms of the colonial era, play their economic game across and between societies. They may produce in one country, distribute through another, and the products may be absorbed in yet a third country. In addition, it is common to find them sending investment money to Third World countries for high yield and to avoid taxes in their own country. National policies are simply more variables to be included in the equation for estimating profits. Multinationals typically do have a disruptive impact on labor and labor relations in Third World countries. The state, rather than local unions, tends to ensure that labor remains co-operative to the demands of multinationals. It is often the case in Third World nations, as in Brazil, that multinationals set up shop because they have been invited by state leaders. In an effort to modernize and develop their own countries, Third World leaders entice them with tax-free profits. However, it is also often the case that the rest of the population of the host country has very little initial interest, motivation or attachment to the new production apparatus. Because of their economic and political stature, multinationals superimpose an historically and culturally different form of social organization on the host country. In effect, multinationals overlay a social organization which arranges human activity along different temporal and spatial lines while the old form of organization still retains some of its influence.

It should not be thought that disjunctures of space and time, and hence moral/political realms, take place only, or primarily, between the economic core and peripheral nations (MacIntyre, 1981). Within core nations, change in one sphere of society does not necessarily entail uniform change in other spheres: 'it is overwhelmingly unlikely that any institutions developed by human mind will be able to accommodate indefinitely and efficiently any new economic and technological changes that happen to come along' (Hirschman, 1971, p. 23). In the realm of ideas, for example, it is not at all clear that scientific beliefs dominate Western culture. One need not be an astute observer to see that religious beliefs, astrology, folk wisdom, common sense, and witchcraft remain common forms of explanation in modern societies. Nor are these forms solely at the fringes. Highly technical, scientific weapons and military organizations interact in a frightening way with political ideology, so that we can never be sure if non-scientific beliefs will ignite the scientific-technological military apparatus.

Modern societies reveal disjunctures of space and time in other ways. Various ethnic groups, for instance, choose to perpetuate older forms of social organization which interact with the present. Religious institutions choose a moral vocabulary and behavior patterns laid down thousands of years ago. From a sociological point of view, this means that modern societies do not function or maintain themselves simply in the present. To a large degree, the problems and contradictions of modern societies are based on ruptures in both spatial and temporal zones. The American Indians fight in modern courts of law for tribal land originally belonging to their ancestors. Contemporary religious wars in the Middle East, fought with methods and techniques from alien cultures, exemplify the contradictions. As Shils points out, the veneer of modernity is often thin.

In the new states of Asia and Africa, traditional ideals, beliefs, attachments and practices have not yet yielded to the rather feeble rationalizing exertions of their rulers. Nigeria, for example, broke down in the conflict of interests and beliefs of several major ethnic and religious communities. The conflict was in part a conflict of interests in the anticipated advantages to be obtained through control of the federal government over appointments and the allocation of funds to regions. But the collectivities themselves were defined by traditions of belief and attachment. In India, the battle of castes and regions over the allocation of appointments, opportunities to obtain the educational qualification for appointments, and the allocation of federal funds to regions is sustained, indeed, would be impossible without the prior definition of the contending collectivities by traditions of belief about the caste system and the theology from which it is derived ... The recurrent outbursts of violence between Tamils and Singhalese in Sri Lanka are of similar origin; the long-standing conflicts between the Christian South Sudanese and the Muslim government of the Sudan are likewise products of these intertwined interests and traditions of belief and attachment. In the communist countries, the increasing resistance of the peasantry to the communist rationalization of agriculture is still another manifestation of the power of intertwined interest and traditions of belief and attachment to resist the unrelenting rationalizing schemes. (Shils, 1981, p. 301)

For many actors the choice of the past over the present is outweighed only by the hope for the future (Kerblay, 1983).

Finally, ruptures in modern society are often caused by anticipation of the future, as well as choice selections from the past, and create new conflicts not necessarily reducible to class divisions.[4]

The ecologists have extended the critique of industrial technology beyond its immediate effects upon human health and other forms of life by raising the questions of the long term impact of scientifically- and technologically-based culture. Advanced ecological thinking demands that the concept of life be extended to the biosphere, whose rhythms are autonomous from human intervention and must be obeyed in order to sustain our forms of life. This is a proposal to 'humanize' nature as a concrete scientific category. (Aronowitz, 1981, p. 81)

New social movements, with the future as their guide, have caused ruptures and cracks in modern society that are not simply based on producing a specific kind of social organization. They are often outcomes of the actors' sense of their own historicity (Touraine, 1983). In these movements, the temporal (future) self-consciousness of the actors is extremely high. For example, the women's movement suggests that male oppression may be a transhistorical phenomenon; and some women wonder whether the economic reorganization of society will be of any use to their historical situation. To reinvigorate sociological theory, then, requires that several changes be made in the current project. Theories which seek a master principle relating human nature and society may be seeking the unattainable: coherence between self and society is itself problematic, and the social issues of today only emphasize that fact.

Conclusion: Self, Society and Moral Discourse

The early history of sociology was replete with individuals who, in different countries and at different times, declared that if the program of sociology were followed all, or most, of society's problems would be solved. As Durkheim (1938) argued, only sociologists were capable of detecting the essential aspects of human activity. In my view, this optimistic attitude was based on two related notions: (1) classical sociologists often believed they had unlocked *the major principle, structure or characteristic of modern society*, and (2) consequently, having discovered the central problem, they only needed a master discourse (sociology) to provide a solution.[5] Modern societies exhibit spatial and temporal unevenness in their structures suggesting this is no longer a viable theoretical approach. A great many conflicts, therefore, are due to contemporary actors choosing, and acting, in different temporal arenas of moral/political meaning.

In my view, classical sociological theory, as well as most contemporary work, reduces the self and society to amoral master principles. The self is reduced to a set of ahistorical drives in which the moral actor disappears into the various characteristics offered to describe modern societies. Only an alternative view of the actor (cf. Gewirth, 1978) and society permits us to see the moral self. This view suggests that modern societies do not hang together very well and that the moral cracks and crevices are exactly what the actor has to negotiate. Individuals, in so far as they are shaped by social influences and bounded by body and memory, often respond to more than one type of moral and political discourse. In sum, the problems that an individual faces today may be significantly different from those of one's neighbor.

If this view is plausible, one possible role for sociology is to help individuals steer a moral course through the manifold fissures of modern society. Since sociology is inevitably a form of moral discourse, it defines itself in relation to other types of moral discourse available to the individual. For the most part, sociology has borrowed the rhetoric and vocabulary of Enlightenment thought and its concomitant optimism. Thinkers of the Enlightenment expected easy solutions to the problem of the individual in relation to society. They wrongly presumed that either we need society to control the impulsive aspects of human nature or we must adjust our society (that is, some part of it) to get the right types of individuals.

Present theories of society are encumbered by these old ideologies. One direction for sociology today would be to learn from the new social movements, such as the peace movement, the environmental movement and the women's movement. This is *not* to say that it should become the ideology of these movements. Rather, sociology should critically examine both the *limits* of new ideologies and moral perspectives, and their *potential* to bring about a new and better social order.

Notes

I would like to thank Robert L. Johnson, Mark L. Wardell and Nicholas C. Mullins for numerous helpful comments and suggestions.

1   I develop this argument and related ones in more detail and at great length in an unpublished book manuscript, *The Transformation of Self and Society.*

2   In my view there are two additional answers, language/cognition and exchange processes, both having ancient lineages. Because of spatial limitations, these will not be discussed.

3   The moral and political realms are often closely linked; see Taylor, 1982. The fact that individuals may act for political/moral reasons not reducible to psychology or social psychology has recently been noted by some biographers/intellectual historians. Consult, for example, Crick's, 1980, refusal to reduce Orwell's political acts to something less than they were.

4   Aronowitz, 1981, p. 116, argues that Marxism is 'seriously flawed' in its conception of social time. It 'cannot integrate the nonsynchronous into its dialectical conception of history'. For him (p. 117), 'Unevenness, then, is not merely a *spatial* category related to conditions of capital accumulation; it is also a *temporal* category ... For groups whose struggles are rooted in various moments of time, in different political and cultural problematics associated with these moments, the problematic of class may or not be the effect of their struggles'.

5   The work of C. W. Mills is simply the exception that proves the rule.

6

The Concept of Structure in Sociology

David Rubinstein

The most durable candidate for a foundation stone for a science of society is the concept of social structure.[1] But the concept remains vaguely and variously defined. Sometimes structures are physical variables such as size, density and propinquity. Other structural variables are cognitive, some normative, like kinship, and others non-normative, such as friendship choices. There are also mixed cases, such as heterogeneity, which consists in the physical (or cognitive) mixing of normatively (or non-normatively) defined categories. A heterogeneous neighborhood made up of Protestants and Catholics describes both cognitive (normative) and physical mixing. An office comprised of friends and strangers is a non-normative cognitive and physical mix. In so far as size consists of a count of units cognitively defined (such as the number of Democrats in the room) it can be a similarly mixed variable. Further, some structural variables are theory-dependent. Power and stratification are conceptualized differently by rival theories and hence cannot be identified apart from a specific theoretical orientation. Terms like 'activity patterns' or 'the complex array of roles and statuses' or 'socio-historical conditions' might consist in any or all of the various dimensions of structure. A survey of structural variables quickly reveals a conceptual grab bag of importantly different kinds of things.

Among the progenitors of the concept, Marx, Durkheim and Simmel are usually singled out as the most important. Marx's distinction between 'social existence' and 'consciousness', and his claim that 'Society does not consist of individuals, but expresses the sum of interrelations in which individuals stand with respect to one another', nicely express basic elements of structural thought. Durkheim's (1938, p. 112) description of social facts as 'ways of thinking, acting, and feeling external to the individual and endowed with a power of coercion' and his claim that social phenomena 'vary ... according to the ways in which the constituent parts of society are grouped' are commonly identified as distinctively structural concepts. Simmel's formal sociology, because it stresses patterns of relations abstracted from their 'contents', and his emphasis on numbers, have been incorporated by structural sociologists.

Amid the vague and conceptually idiosyncratic definitions of structure, a distinctive meta-theoretical current is visible. While structural variables may include cognitive factors, structures are often conceived as 'objective' features of social organization that exist apart from culture and the consciousness of participating actors, that is, as elements of social organization constraining belief and action identifiable by the social scientist but unknown to social actors. The sharp line drawn between the ideas of ordinary actors and the concept of structure seems clear in Marx's (1967, p. 14) distinction between the 'phantoms formed in the human brain' and 'their material life-process'. Durkheim (1938, p. 32) similarly claims that 'the social scientist must emancipate himself from the fallacious ideas that dominate the mind of the layman'. Indeed, Durkheim praised Marx for his distinction between 'the notions of those who participate in [social life]' and 'the manner according to which the associated individuals are grouped' (quoted in Winch, 1958, p. 23).

Contemporary definitions of structure often parallel this ambition. Echoing Simmel, Peter Blau (1974, p. 616) defines social structures as 'population distributions among social positions'. He claims that in his concept of structure 'formal properties of social positions and relations are abstracted from their substantive contents, notably from cultural and psychological orientations' (Blau, 1977, p. 28). He also asserts that 'most structural sociologists distinguish the cultural realm of ideas and ideals from the structural realm of different positions and patterns of relations' (Blau, 1981, p. 21). Similarly, Duncan and Schnore (1959, p. 137) describe social structure as 'activity constellations' and 'patterns of activity' and claim that the 'notion of subjective obligation emphasized in role theory is irrelevant for our purposes'. They insist that 'the individual's personal view of things is, as such, of no ecological interest' (Duncan and Schnore, 1959, p. 142).

The most recent and self-conscious attempt to establish sociology on aggregate variables that can be identified independently of actors' ideas is network theory. For these theorists, a proper sociology would consist in the study of the interactions of units (such as individuals, villages, societies), and the interactions they are interested in are those that are not normatively prescribed, as White, Boorman and Breiger (1976, p. 733) put it: 'the network of interstices that exist outside the normative constructs and the attribute breakdowns of our everyday categories'. They reject the emphasis of conventional role theory on 'subjective perceptions by the parties which are at once very difficult to establish and often not relevant to the objective structure' (White, Boorman and

Breiger, 1976, p. 1391), and argue that 'the kind of role structures which interest us here are descriptions of actual overall structure not accessible to any unaided observer' (p. 1389). White, Boorman and Breiger focus on unrecognized networks in the belief that they promise greater explanatory power than normative networks. To this end, 'The cultural and social-psychological meanings of actual ties are largely bypassed' (White, Boorman and Breiger, 1976, p. 734). They claim (p. 1388) that kinship systems are not to be taken as descriptions of structures but as 'brilliant ideologies of social structure'.

Bruce Mayhew argues that a proper sociology consists exclusively in the study of aggregate structures that are independent of the consciousness of social members. In this view, structures, like communication and authority networks, must be understood in terms of 'how the network is organized and on nothing else' (Mayhew, 1980, p. 344). Mayhew (p. 349) further claims that genuinely sociological analysis is indifferent to the properties of individuals: 'In structural sociology the unit of analysis is always the social network, *never the individual*.' It is the organization of units, not their individual characteristics, that is the proper concern of sociology, for 'structuralists study organization, not people' and believe that 'from the point of view of social organization all individuals are interchangeable' (Mayhew, 1980, p. 349). Mayhew's aversion to the incorporation of members' ideas into the structural conception of social organization results in a radical behaviorism. He (1980, pp. 348, 363–4) claims that 'structuralists do not employ subjectivist concepts such as purpose or goals' and aims at expunging all reference to 'ghostly' or 'subcranial' properties such as 'values', 'purpose'¨ and 'attitudes, emotions, sentiments, etc.'. He considers these factors to be, at best, individualistic in their reference or, at worst, perpetuating a 'demono-logical perspective' more appropriate to 'witchdoctors' than scientists. Oddly, Mayhew (1980, p. 347) goes on to include 'symbol systems organized into social ideologies' as a structural variable. Duncan and Schnore (1959, p. 151) similarly exclude 'mutual understandings and consensual meanings' from social explanation: 'the concept of social organization set forth in our paper does not involve such subjective elements'.

If elements of subjective experience are accorded any place in structural theory, they are treated as epiphenomenal, as dependent variables to be accounted for in terms of the more causally efficacious facts of social structure. According to Durkheim (1966, p. 226): 'mental representa-tions function above all as an expression of a reality not of their own making ... Religious conceptions are the products of the social environment, rather than its producers'. Schnore (1958, p. 632) describes Durkheim's treatment of 'shared norms and values ... as mere "emanations" of underlying social morphology or structure'. White, Boorman and Breiger (1976, p. 1390) deny 'that norms determine role behavior' and suggest that norms and cultural roles 'are patterns emergent from concrete networks among particular persons'.

The ultimate purpose of structural theorists is typically to replicate the format of the natural sciences by finding variables that can apply across a broad range of social settings and explain social process in terms of general laws. Jonathan Turner (1979, p. 453) describes his quest for a 'social physics' as: 'to uncover the basic and generic properties of the social world and to articulate these properties as a series of abstract principles'. This goal is equally clear in the work of the other modern-day structuralists in the United States.

My comments here have drawn selectively on the great range of conceptions of structure. The behaviorism and positivism of the theorists cited are by no means universal. Many uses of the term structure are theoretically much 'softer' in that they consider cultural or subjective factors, like norms and role expectations, to be structural, and are not aimed at creating laws of social process. But the critique of social science offered by advocates of the hard conception of structure applies to its soft version; the imprecision of the soft concepts precludes general explanatory laws and their dependence on the subjectivity of social actors suggests that they remain individualistic and psychological. Also, one of the aims of the structural approach is to show the dependent and epiphenomenal nature of norms, and this explanatory goal is precluded by their inclusion in the definition of structures. It is the reasonableness of the hard concept of structure that is at issue here.

The purpose of this essay is to show that this program for a social science is impossible and in fact was betrayed by its own advocates. In the following sections I will argue that the promise of general theory is compromised with the use of concepts far too vague to support this hope. I will then show that the attempt to cut social theory loose from the concepts of social actors fails and that assertions about structural relations rely implicitly on assumptions about intentional actions. In the conclusion, I shall comment on the extra-theoretical motives behind the structuralist program for a social science.

Structure and General Theory

Perhaps the first question to be raised about the concept of structure is whether its primary ambition can actually be achieved, that is, whether the variables offered can have the explanatory potential claimed. The positivist goal of explanatory parsimony is clear in Durkheim's (1938, p. 114) claim that 'the number of social units' and 'dynamic density' are the basic explanatory elements of sociology. Similarly, Blau focuses on a handful of variables such as size, heterogeneity and degree of status differentiation, which are purported to have great explanatory power. Blau (1981, p. 13) at times suggests that size alone is a kind of keystone variable around which a good deal of social theory might be built. Mayhew (1980, p. 339) speaks of the variables which define 'population, environment, ideological and technological subsystems' and he asserts that 'for structuralists, a general sociological theory is a set of theorems stated in terms of these variables, theorems which will predict and explain the structure and dynamics of societal phenomena' – an enterprise Mayhew considers to be 'coextensive with sociology itself'. J. Turner (1979, p. 446) offers twelve principles of the processes of differentiation, integration, distingegration and interaction which he believes will provide 'a solid foundation for sociological theorizing'.

There has been of course extensive debate on whether it is reasonable to seek a general theory in the social sciences. Some have claimed that the unique histories of social units, which cannot be incorporated as structural variables, are essential to their understanding. In addition, if the effect of a structural variable must be mediated through a particular culture, its explanatory power and range would be reduced. And the fact that the human systems are not closed limits the potential of general laws. If the effects of crowding in Amsterdam and Calcutta cannot be described independently of the particular history and unique cultures of these cities, and if both are penetrated by external systems, we cannot explain the effects of crowding in terms of general laws. Surely the effects of another of Blau's favorite variables, racial heterogeneity, are quite different in Hawaii than in South Africa.

It is difficult to preclude the possibility that structural variables might some day be incorporated into a general theory of social process; impossibility arguments are the most difficult to make. But it can be shown that structuralists are more successful with the rhetoric than the substance of general theory. A *sine qua non* of general theory is conceptual clarity and parsimony. But only the illusion of these desiderata can be found in structural theory. For example, Mayhew faults an exchange theorist for including eleven variables in the explanation of action and he derides subjectivism and 'individualism' for their obscurantist insistence on the complexity of human behavior. But his claim that structural sociology can achieve theoretical parsimony is not sustained. For while Mayhew centers his discussion on variables like the division of labor, the degree of stratification, and networks of authority and communication, this apparent precision is lost in Mayhew's master list of the most salient features of social organization: population, environment and ideological and technical sub-systems. These subjects are so diffuse as to allow the incorporation of almost anything, and Mayhew provides no hint of their precise definition. 'Population' and so forth are subject matters, not merely 'aspects of social organization'. I cannot imagine what he might mean, or *not* mean, by 'environment'. Thus Mayhew has revealed the difficulty of achieving general theory vis-à-vis structural variables by using terms which reintroduce the vagueness and fluidity which his conception of structure purports to remedy.

This expansion of the range of explanatory factors amid the rhetoric of general theory is common. Durkheim describes the 'forms of association' as 'number' and 'dynamic density'. But he then defines dynamic density as the number of individuals who have social relations and 'live a common life' (Durkheim, 1938, p. 114). The openness and vagueness of this 'structural' variable enriches Durkheim's approach, but only by sacrificing his positivist aspirations. Similarly, Duncan and Schnore (1959) center their discussion on an austere selection of structural variables, like size, degree of differentiation, and internal stratification. But, in apparent recognition of the explanatory paucity of these sorts of variables, they describe their approach as centered on 'four main referential concepts; population, environment, technology, and organiza- tion, which define what may be called the "ecological complex"' (Duncan and Schnore, 1959, p. 136). Like Durkheim and Mayhew, Duncan and Schnore promise the theoretical parsimony of general theory but then open up their explanatory terms to incorporate whatever might be included as an element of, for example, 'organization' or 'environment'. Population and technology are subject matters, not variables, and a deductive general theory must be framed in terms of variables, not subject matters.

Structural sociologists aim at replicating Marx and Durkheim's method, but their approach is quite different. The mode of production is a far more comprehensive 'variable' than size, heterogeneity, and so forth. Marx used the term to describe an entire form of life that encompassed many facets of social organization and process; and he frequently disavowed pretentions to a Comtean science of society.[2] While Durkheim's methodological statements do seem to take positivism seriously, in his substantive work he also depicts a complex form of life that cannot be rendered into the handful of variables suggested by structural sociologists.

Moreover, Marx and Durkheim's work differs from that of contemporary structuralists in that they offer comprehensive theories that justify their choice of variables. In Marx's case, for example, his theory of society begins with the notion of production and, hence, mode of production can be justified as an important, if not central, concept on the basis of an integrative logic concerning production. In contrast, we are provided with little theoretical rationale for the salience of size, heterogeneity, and so forth – little reason to believe that they are uniquely explanatory. The arbitrariness and abstractness of the variables of contemporary structuralists suggest the appropriateness of multivariate analysis, but a skein of disconnected variables does not make 'the beginning of a scientific revolution' that Berkowitz (1981, p. 150) promises.

Objective Structures and the Subjectivity of the Actor

The most striking, and perhaps the defining, feature of hard structuralism is its attempt to define structures independently of culture and psychology. The avoidance of cognitive elements is motivated by the belief that they are necessarily individual and hence not properly sociological. It is also felt that the subjective is essentially interior and hence inaccessible to scientific scrutiny. Thirdly, the positivist canon that scientific theory must be rooted in so-called 'brute data', or data that can simply be observed and that do not require interpretation, encourages avoidance of culture and psychology.[3]

In describing their ecological version of structural analysis, Duncan and Schnore (1959, p. 137), for example, claim 'the ecologist is interested in the pattern of observable physical activity itself rather than the subjective expectations that individuals may entertain of their roles'. Blau (1977, p. 28) aims to discover 'what independent influence the structure of social positions in a society or community exerts on social relations' and by this he means 'independently of cultural values and psychological motives'. White, Boorman and Breiger (1976, p. 734 n.) claim: 'the delineation of concrete social structure should be analytically divorced from symbolic and cultural analysis'. When structural theorists incorporate the subjective it is as an object of explanation, not as a medium requiring some independent consideration. This shunting of cognitive elements from structural variables, then, can be found throughout the work of structural theorists.

The attempt to side-step the cultural categories of social members, it would seem, must fail because most sociologically significant groupings are constituted with cognitive elements. Mayhew cannot describe 'how the network is organized' independently of the organizing principles used by social members, particularly if these are networks of authority and communication. This is not to say that all social networks are cognized by the actors or culturally dictated. But even the 'invisible' (to the actors) relations, the focus of network theory, emerge from cognitive properties of subjects, such as 'liking', 'knowing'. This inter-penetration of social structure with cognitive elements can be found throughout the variables preferred by structuralists. Blau (1974, p. 620) claims that 'values' and 'cultural traditions' and 'norms' are not part of social structure. He (1977) also believes that variables such as status, ethnicity, kinship and authority are structural, but it would be impossible to discuss any of these variables abstracted from all 'cultural and psychological orientations'. Blau's move is common among structural theorists; elements of culture and consciousness are theoretically excluded and then smuggled back in through substantive concepts.

Mayhew, among others, believes that the division of labor and systems of stratification can be defined independently of subjective elements. But the division of labor is a system of intentional actions unified by a purpose. And a system of stratification must include an array of factors, like prestige, status, and authority which certainly implicate attitudes, sentiments, and beliefs. Mayhew includes 'symbol systems organized into social ideologies' as a legitimate structural concern. He also speaks of 'cultural information' and 'authority' as elements in structural analysis. But rather than explaining how these referents avoid the 'mental' contents he seeks to exclude, Mayhew (1980, p. 347) simply wraps them in computer terminology: 'the biological memory banks of humans ... the external memory banks of material culture' [for example, books and paintings]. Mayhew considers ideology to be a structural variable. How to include ideology, but not the proscribed 'goals', 'purposes', and 'values' is not explained.

Duncan and Schnore believe that their notion of social structure can underwrite a general sociology. They contend that 'the salient features of a bureaucracy are its great size, its high degree of differentiation, and its internal stratification – properties of the aggregate itself' (Duncan and Schnore, 1959, p. 138). But differentiation and stratification surely implicate the role definitions of organizational members which Duncan and Schnore consider 'irrelevant'. It would be difficult even to define bureaucracy apart from norms of universalism, and surely goals and purposes are essential to its understanding. Since a bureaucracy is a uniquely intentional organization, that is, deliberately formed, it would be especially difficult to describe apart from the consciousness of its members. None of this entails that a bureaucracy can be fully explained vis-à-vis members' consciousness. But even 'size', Blau's master variable, does not have 'unambiguous operational meaning' (Blau, 1981, p. 13) for it must be determined by members' often very ambiguous rules of inclusion.

Duncan and Schnore speak of social structure as 'patterns of activity' which they consider to be identifiable independently of culture. But this claim suggests a profound misunderstanding of the nature of social action. Social actions, like signaling and voting, only exist within a network of institutionalized norms and values, that is, the 'consensual meanings and mutual understandings' Duncan and Schnore aim at excluding. The action of raising one's hand constitutes 'voting' only in terms of a context of norms and values and hence it is 'consensual meanings and mutual understandings' that distinguish voting from a Strangelovian twitch.

Granovetter's landmark article, 'The strength of weak ties', offers propositions about the effects of structural arrangements that reveal similar difficulties in excluding cognitive elements. He claims that a strong tie between A and B and A and C virtually ensures that there will be a comparably strong tie between B and C. If A is strongly tied to B and C, Granovetter (1973, p. 1363), avowedly overstating the case, claims that 'the [forbidden] triad *never* occurs'. But his proposition simply does not hold independently of specific attitudinal or cultural contents. If A is a man, B his wife, and C his mistress, A certainly, and B and C probably, will make considerable efforts to see that B and C develop no tie. This example shows the danger in establishing abstract structural propositions independently of the specific character of the relationships. In Simmel's terms, 'contents' are essentially involved in determining 'forms'. Indeed, the very definition of a triad, as opposed to three contiguous bodies, consists in members' self definitions and mutual orientations.

Network theorists are particularly emphatic that social actors' cognitive categories must be superseded by behavioral redescriptions derived from the study of patterned interactions. Berkowitz (1981, pp. 14, 25) advocates that we 'derive definitions of groups from an analysis of patterns of relations among elements' rather than from 'individual consciousness or internal states of mind'. Surely it is not just 'patterns of relations', but the ideas of social members that define ethnicity, organizational positions, and occupations. Structural theorists have shown little appreciation for the extravagance of their advocacy that members' categories be superseded by observationally based categories. As debate on abortion and brain death illustrate, the very concept of a living human being is a matter of social definition. While 'relational analysis' might be relevant to these controversies, it is preposterous to think that the ideas of social members could be irrelevant in the definition of social categories.

Simmel is often cited as a pioneer of structural analysis, but he argued forcefully that the social scientific idea of society necessarily involved ideas in society. He contrasted nature and society in Kantian terms arguing that, while nature must be 'synthesized' by an observing subject, society is, as it were, pre-synthesized by its own constituents (Simmel, 1965, p. 338).

The concept of structure as an external, objective and controlling system is also purported to be compatible with Marxism. But Marx

(1964, p. 158) considered the concept of social order as a system of objective structures somehow distinct from, and controlling of, human consciousness and action to be a prime case of reification. 'It is above all necessary to avoid postulating "society" once again as an abstraction confronting the individual.' For example, very little can be said about an economy without taking into account the legal system which constitutes its essential elements: ownership, sales, rights and contracts. As Renner (1949, p. 59) put it, 'legal and economic institutions, though not identical, are but two aspects of the same thing, inextricably interwoven'. Marx argued further that formal law is parasitic on the capitalist mode of production, but the latter cannot be prior to all elements of culture or 'consciousness'. This dependence of an economic system on cultural conventions extends to the very 'forces of production'. A waterfall has no economic significance unless it is *defined* as a force of production; super-structural elements are implicated in the so-called sub-structure. In fact, Marx (1964, p. 158) claimed that it is only in alienated conditions that 'The social character of activity appears here as an alien object in relation to the individuals ... their mutual relationship appears to the individuals themselves as something alien and autonomous, as an object.'

Structures and Actions

As indicated above, structural sociologists insist on explaining action in structural terms and hence reject altogether explanations framed in terms of intentions and purposes. Arguing from his belief 'that all regular actors in positions in organizations are alike (in other words, that personal biography makes little difference in what they do)', Charles Warriner (1981, pp. 187–8) contends that 'acts are structured by and triggered into performance in terms of the position the actor is in'. For the behaviorist, subjective explanation of action is founded on 'ghostly' (Mayhew) entities. But while structuralist explanations stating relationships between aggregate variables may avoid overt reference to culture in the formulation of structural concepts, structural sociologists cannot avoid implicit assumptions about intentional actions.

This is brought out in Stephen Turner's (1977) critique of Blau's theory of differentiation. Aiming to create a general theory of structure that 'ignores the psychological forces that govern individual behavior' (Blau, 1970, pp. 203, 213) asserts that 'the large size of an organization indirectly raises the ratio of administrative personnel through the structural differentiation it generates'. Blau (1970, p. 203) believes that the relationship between these organizational variables can be stated 'without investigating the motives of the individuals in organizations'. But Turner shows that the relationships Blau describes are parasitic on the practical reasoning of social actors. For, as Blau obliquely admits, the increase in the ratio of administrative personnel is consciously chosen by organizational members and hence 'the patterns that Blau's generalizations cover hold only in virtue of the fact that organizational participants act in certain ways for certain reasons' (Turner, 1977, p. 18). Turner considers the possibility of a legislative enactment that regulated the ratio of administrative personnel. Noting that it is an odd sort of scientific law that a legislature can repeal, Turner (1977, p. 28) argues that 'the aggregate patterns of relations between the variable of size and the "differentiation" variables would necessarily have been changed as a consequence of this change in practice. This means that the pattern holds only if certain kinds of practices – those practices consistent with the pattern – are followed.' Properties of social organization only provide reasons for members to act in certain ways. Persons are not 'propelled by external forces' to increase the ratio of administrative personnel: they decide to. Structural relations depend on the intentions of social actors and the effects of structural variables are thus mediated through the cultural and psychological properties of persons. Like elements of culture, assumptions about intentional actions are theoretically excluded and then smuggled back into explanations that purport to be strictly structural.

Blau's attempt to avoid reference to intentions is typical of structural theory. Mayhew (1980, p. 36) wants to replace 'this *actor* went to his office' with something about 'being propelled from one point to another by forces outside his control'. This is not the place for yet another extended treatment of behaviorism. But Mayhew's example of a behavioral redescription of an intentional action can hardly be encouraging to this program.[4]

Like the attempt to reduce sociological explanation to a handful of structural variables defined independently of culture and psychology, the deletion of intentional action is justified in terms of the classics of sociology. But again, this depends on a selective reading, for there is much in Marx, Simmel and Durkheim to suggest that intentional action, like culture, is essential to their understanding of social process. Nevertheless, some support for the various doctrines of hard structuralism can be found in all three theorists. Marx and Durkheim especially were captivated by the success of natural science and tempted to imitate its methods, which seemed to dictate an objectivist model of social explanation. But, unlike contemporary structuralists, neither could avoid a profound ambivalence about this program. In Marx's case, structural determinism contradicted his commitment to revolutionary praxis and to the possibility of ultimate human freedom. Durkheim's essentially conservative concern for normative consensus, and its unraveling in modern society, prevented an unequivocal acceptance of materialistic structuralism. As scientists, Marx and Durkheim sought to reduce social explanation to a handful of deterministic structural variables. But as moral philosophers they needed to retain a vision of man as a conscious actor and a cultural being. The methodological ambivalence of both Marx and Durkheim was thus sustained by the tension between their political and scientific commitments. The hard structuralist reading of Marx and Durkheim by contemporary sociologists emerges from a resolution of this tension. As will be argued in the next section, political considerations do not restrain, and in fact encourage, the hard structuralism of contemporary sociology.

Meta-theoretical Roots

There are numerous implausibilities in the program of hard structuralism. The hopes that social science can be reduced to a handful of structural variables, that these variables can be defined independently of culture and psychology, and that social process can be explained without reference to intentional action are all routinely contradicted within the work of structural sociologists.

Positivism has become a popular whipping boy for those dissatisfied with mainstream sociology, nevertheless the bizarre aspirations of structural sociology are inconceivable apart from this legacy. The quest for general laws of social process is of course positivist. The attempt to conceive structural variables independently of culture and psychology is too. General laws require the identification of variables that can apply cross-culturally and trans-historically. Such variables must be defined independently of specific cultural contents, for cultural variables are inherently idiosyncratic, or idiographic, and a generalizing, or nomothetic, science must be rooted in factors that are independent of the variety of cultures. Any group or society can be described in terms of size, the division of labor, or the degree of inequality, and if social theory can be framed in terms of these variables the prospects of general theory are enhanced, particularly if these variables can be defined 'objectively'. But if unique cultural contents must be incorporated, either in the choice of explanatory variables or in their formulation, generality is diminished. If, for example, population density has a different 'meaning' in a prison than a college dormitory, if the effects of crowding are mediated through the culturally shaped consciousness of social actors, the generality of abstract principles on the effects of crowding is diminished. This is why Weber's skepticism about the possibility of general laws in social science was associated with an emphasis on the role of culture, for instance, in the rise of capitalism.

Demonstrating the resilience and relative autonomy of culture would require a review of a vast and controversial literature, but it is clear that the attempt of structural theorists to supersede culture and psychology by demonstrating the causal priority and explanatory sufficiency of structural variables has met with little success. The promise of a strictly structural sociology has remained a background ambition that waxes and wanes as new formulations appear. Warriner believes 'that personal biography makes little difference'. Mayhew claims that 'all individuals are interchangeable' and that a sociology indifferent to 'values' and 'purposes' is a real possibility. Blau purports to ignore 'cultural and psychological orientations', and White, Boorman and Breiger too ignore 'normative constructs' and 'subjective perceptions'. Duncan and Schnore suggest that norms will prove to be mere 'emanations' of structure and White, Boorman and Breiger argue that kinship systems are just 'ideologies'. But disappointment is the usual result of this extravagant ambition. Indeed, this disappointment is evident in the theorists cited in this essay whose ambition is to get sociology finally on track as a predictive science by indentifying the appropriate structural variables.

There is, however, a second impetus to the program of hard structuralism other than establishing sociology as a predictive science. The emphasis on the determinative power of structural variables is uniquely suited to a program of social engineering. If human action and belief are epiphenomenal, if they are constrained by structural arrangements, then modification of those arrangements becomes a lever with which action and belief can be manipulated. The structural perspective is uniquely suited to an engineering impulse because it promises a form of social change that can be indifferent to culture since culture is conceived as a manipulable 'emanation'. The ordinary person cherishes culture, but is ignorant of its 'causes', which the social science expert knows how to manipulate.

The idea of human malleability was central to the Enlightenment. Despite a recognition of the impact of 'materialist' factors that constrain society (for example, the number of people or the division of labor) in Montesquieu, the main focus of the philosophes was on the reform of consciousness and culture through education. But there was an undercurrent of thought that focused on the manipulation of institutional arrangements, rather than the enlightenment of persons, as a means of effecting social change. This belief that techniques of social engineering would obviate the need to reshape persons was most evident in early modern political thought which aimed at discovering forms of political organization that would resist the deficiencies of human character (see Wolin, 1960, ch. 10). Eventually, the engineering approach won out over re-educative programs, in part because of the stubborn loyalty people displayed towards their culture and in part because the technologically oriented scientist is not as well suited to the transformation of belief, the natural domain of the priest, as to the manipulation of structures.

While Marx was not immune to the temptations of social engineering, his third thesis on Feuerbach criticized the program of using circumstances as a means of manipulating persons:

> The materialist doctrine that men are products of circumstances and upbringing and that, therefore, changed men are products of other circumstances and changed upbringing, forgets that it is men that change circumstances and that the educator himself needs educating. Hence, this doctrine necessarily arrives at dividing society into two parts, of which one is superior to society (in Robert Owen, for example).

These charges of theoretical incoherence and elitism apply well to the program of structural sociology. The beliefs 'that all individuals are interchangeable', that 'cultural and psychological orientations' do not matter, suggest that the social engineer, who somehow escapes the determination that governs ordinary people, can safely ignore the preferences and purposes of social members. Without a moral vision like Marx's or Durkheim's, the dream of a science of human behavior can quickly become a dream of social control. From the perspective of hard structuralism, persons are passive products of circumstances, and human consciousness is a mere shadow that can be readily recast. What people want and believe is a remediable obstacle.

Conclusion

The failure of hard structuralism as a scientific program tells us something about the prospects of manipulated reform. Despite promises of its irrelevance, culture has proved to be a significant category of social explanation. The failure of structural sociology to reduce culture to successfully explained dependent variables, and to identify the structural variables through which it can be manipulated, is paralleled by a failure of the program to change persons by changing circumstances. Historical cultures have a way of *not* collapsing when their alleged structural supports are removed. The past continues to weigh on the minds of the living. Structural sociology has promised us a lever with which people who resist 'education' can be changed anyway. All too often disappointment in the effectiveness of this non-coercive lever has led to the use of a coercive means of social change. The relative autonomy of culture from circumstance, and the ways in which culture is built into the very concept of structure, partially explain the practical and conceptual failures of even the more coercive programs. A greater respect for the integrity of culture might be an antidote for both the theoretical extravagance of structural sociologists and the arrogance of the social engineer.

Notes

1   The concept of 'structure' to be examined here is confined to the term as used in, largely, American sociology. While it bears some resemblance to the 'structuralism' of various European disciplines, the similarity is superficial. The superficiality of the parallel is argued by Michael Lane, 1970, p. 36. Blau, 1981, p. 18, believes the term structure can usefully overarch psychoanalysis and behaviorism, Parsons and ecological sociology.
2   There are numerous points at which Marx repudiates the ideas of positivism. Responding to an admirer's attempt to find universal laws in his work, Marx, 1965b, p. 22, says: 'He has to transform my sketch of the origins of capitalism in Western Europe into an historical-philosophical theory of universal movement necessarily imposed on all people, no matter what the historical circumstances in which they are placed ... But I must protest. He does me too much honour, and at the same time discredits me.'
3   Charles Taylor, 1971, describes the role of 'brute data' in natural science and its unavailability in social science.
4   A counter-argument to behaviorism that occasionally turns up in the literature is a model of simplicity but carries decisive force. Mayhew has written an article with the *purpose* of changing our *minds* in the *belief* that this will make a difference. The very articulation of this position effectively refutes it. In discussing the practice of modern sociology, Mayhew uses the following 'ghostly' terms: bias, insight, interest, perspicacity, intellectual assumptions.

7

The Dissolution of the Social?

Scott Lash and John Urry

In this chapter we will consider a radicalized version of the claim that sociological theory is in a process of dissolution. We will explore the issue whether 'the social' itself is in a state of collapse; or, more precisely, whether the social – as conceived by social theory – is in a process of disintegration. Here we will consider several recent developments which have re-introduced the actor, or agency, onto social theoretical centre stage. Although these approaches exhibit considerable differences, they nevertheless represent a substantial shift in theory away from the structurally deterministic approaches especially common in Western Europe in the 1970s. And while each of these contemporary developments suffers from considerable problems, they enable us to interrogate and problematize the 'social' in ways which had not previously been possible. The new 'imperialism' of theories of social action has pushed back the boundaries of the social in several important ways. First, causality is partly displaced from social structure onto agency. Second, contradiction is displaced from structure onto agency, in so far as agents bring about social contradictions, or contradiction becomes a quality of action (rather than structure) itself. Third, what were formerly conceived as (for example, cultural, organizational, economic) structures come to be considered as resources which are wielded by collective actors. Fourth, entities such as language and the instincts or libido are no longer located in 'structure', but – without losing their causal powers – are understood as part and parcel of agency. Fifth, resistance to power and domination – indeed often resistance to the social itself – is conceived not so much in regard to structural constraints but in regard to the characteristic of agency itself (cf. Lash, 1984a; Lash and Urry, 1984).

We will now, through the consideration of three rather disparate trends in recent social theory (rational choice theory, game-theoretic Marxism, and French structuralism/post-structuralism), show how the frontiers of the social have been thrust back.

Action as Rational Choice

The starting point for many analyses of the actor in collective action is Olson (1965), through his discussion of the prisoner's dilemma game (see Barry, 1970; Barry and Hardin, 1982; Heath, 1976). The paradox of the game is that if both prisoners pursue their individual self-interest, they end up with a result that is less satisfactory for both than if they had in some way been able to sacrifice those individual interests. This contradiction between what Barry and Hardin call 'Rational Man' (*sic*) and 'Irrational Society' involves a radical critique of rational self-interest. The prisoner's dilemma game demonstrates *contra* Mandeville and Adam Smith that such self-interested action systematically fails to realize the social good (see Elster, 1978, ch. 5).

Olson applies this game to various situations in social life and argues that:

> A lobbying organization, or indeed a labor union or any other organization, working in the interest of a large group of firms or workers in some industry, would get no assistance from the rational, self-interested individuals in that industry. (Olson, 1965, p. 11)

The reason for this derives from the problem of the so-called 'free-rider' in collective action. Where the group to be organized is large and where the benefits from such organization are public and cannot be confined to particular individuals, the group is *latent* and will not become organized unless individuals are induced to co-operate through the provision of other non-collective (selective) incentives. Without such selective benefits, individuals can free-ride, gaining the general benefits of the organization, if any materialize, without incurring any of the material, temporal or motivational costs of membership.

Olson maintains that large groups are likely to remain 'latent' since they have particular problems in establishing and sustaining collective organization. They will be less able to prevent free-riders, particularly because there will be little development of the social pressures and beliefs that would otherwise induce commitment to the organization in question. In a large group not everyone can possibly know everybody else and so each person will not ordinarily be affected if he or she fails to make sacrifices on the group's behalf. Furthermore, the advantages to the whole that each person's potential contribution brings can only be slight, and hence it will not seem worthwhile for a given individual to contribute time, energy or money to the organization in question. At the same time the larger the organization the greater the costs involved in getting it off the ground and into a form whereby any of the collective goods can be obtained. This applies particularly to the problems of mobilizing large-scale social forces, such as social classes.

There are a number of objections to Olson's analysis of rational action. It has been pointed out that 'selective benefits' cannot explain the enormous diversity and strength of actually occurring collective organizations (Barry and Hardin, 1982, pp. 28–9). This is especially relevant for understanding the existence of many groups which do not directly produce any material gains for their members, what Heath terms 'altruistic' pressure groups (Barry, 1970, p. 35; Heath, 1976, p. 126). These groups demand analysis of 'moral incentives' and 'political entrepreneurship' which can partly neutralize the otherwise pervasive free-rider effect (Barry and Hardin, 1982, pp. 29–31).

However, the most serious problem in Olson's analysis concerns the assumption of independent, individual self-interest that is involved. Hardin (1982, pp. 144–55) points out that social life is analogous, not so much to a single-play of prisoner's dilemma, but rather to an iterated prisoner's dilemma or 'supergame'. Where there is iteration, players who should rationally defect (not co-operate), may in fact co-operate. This is because in many social situations people play over time what are in effect a great number of prisoner's dilemma games. They may gradually perceive that, if they pursue their narrow self-interest, they end up with a non-optional collective solution. Hence, there may be a learning process by which many of the actors try out solutions to the games they play which are individually non-rational. And, if these actors come to realize there are major collective gains which result from the pursuit of individually non-rational solutions, these co-operative games may become institutionalized amongst many of the players involved.

Rational choice approaches in politics, especially to explain voting behaviour and the strategies of political parties, have been much discussed. More illuminating than these, however, are the fairly recent attempts to use such notions to analyse wider-ranging contradictions in social and political life. Samuel Brittan (1975), for example, argues that there are two endemic threats to contemporary representative democracy: (1) the generation of excessive expectations; and (2) the disruptive effects of the pursuit of group self-interest in the market-place. He quotes Olson, who maintains that the distinction between privileged and latent groups 'damages the pluralistic view that any outrageous demands of one pressure group will be counterbalanced by the demands of other groups' (Olson, 1965, p. 127). Brittan in particular argues that small sectional groups of trade unionists are increasingly able to mobilize collectively and to alter the distribution of resources. This is because such groups are progressively locked into a competitive struggle. Rival coercive groups in pursuit of self-interest exclude other less organized groups, overload the state, and protect their own place in the national distribution of income and resources. Thus, through their agency, they change the structure. He also argues that there is a noticeable lack of a budget constraint among voters so that people expect too much from government at too little cost. There are excessive expectations generated in which it makes a great deal of sense rationally for politicians to offer more than they can provide. Competition between parties encourages excessive expectations. Moreover, these 'economic contradictions of democracy' have become more significant because of the increasingly obvious lack of any widely shared belief in the legitimacy of the present order. As a consequence Brittan maintains that liberal representative democracy suffers from such internal contradictions that will increase with time, so that the system will, in the not too distant future, disintegrate and disappear.

In Fred Hirsch's (1977) *Social Limits to Growth* the contradictory character of Western democracies is amplified in greater detail via the concept of 'positional goods'. Where such goods dominate the economy, the individually rational and relatively unconstrained demands for higher levels of consumption (as Brittan describes) leads to social irrationality and an eventual undermining of economic development. There are crucial social limits to growth, limits which are as important as physical constraints. These social limits are due to three paradoxes: (1) 'paradox of affluence', or 'why has economic growth remained such a compelling goal to us as individuals even if it yields disappointing fruits when [we] achieve it?'; (2) 'distributional compulsion', or 'why has modern society become so concerned with distribution ... when it is clear that the great majority can raise their living standards only through the production of a larger pie?'; and (3) 'reluctant collectivism', or why has there been 'a universal predominant trend toward collective provision and state regulation in economic areas at a time when individual freedom of action is especially extolled?' (Hirsch, 1977, p. 1). Hirsch tried to explain these paradoxes partly through the disappearance of traditional moral constraints on expectations and desires, but more distinctively through the theory of positional goods.

Goods are 'positional' for Hirsch to the extent that they are characterized by relative scarcity; that is not by physical but by 'social scarcity'. There are, he notes, two types of social scarcity, one in which the satisfaction of a good derives directly from its scarcity, for example in the fashion element or in an antique collection. The second is 'incidental' social scarcity, in which the value of a good declines because of congestion, such as in the case of the individual whose country cottage affords less satisfaction because a whole group of country cottages are built near it. Thus, as the level of average consumption rises, consumption becomes increasingly *social*, that is to say, an individual's satisfaction depends upon that received by others.

Positional goods represent a limitation on the expansion and extension of economic welfare. The increasingly positional nature of goods leads people to a form of 'defensive consumption', whereby individuals have to consume more and more to stay in the same place in the positional economy. Hirsch (1977, p. 49) says of the expansion of educational credentials: 'it is a case of everyone in the crowd standing on tiptoe and no one getting a better view'. The choice facing the individual in a market-type transaction in the positional economy, in a context of material growth, always appears more attractive than it actually turns out after others have exercised their choice (and bought their house in the suburbs, gained their educational credential etc.). Since the market economy is focused upon the wants of individuals in their private isolated capacity these are met. But, because of the increasing significance of positional goods, 'what individuals want and what individually they can get, society cannot get' (Hirsch, 1977, p. 106). Indeed, society will not be able to get this without the development of a social ethic and of collective means which may require implementing individual ends. However, these will be hard to organize, especially because the social limits to growth intensify the distributional struggle and, hence, the importance of relative place. Hirsch summarizes:

> Positional competition has hidden costs for others, and over time for the individual involved; and it intensifies the distributional struggle to a potentially dangerous point. In short, it threatens to displace Smithian harmony by Hobbesian strife and is thereby a dangerous element to leave in the Smithian sector of individualistic optimization. (1977, p. 185)

There are a number of specific difficulties in Hirsch's thesis (see Ellis and Kumar, 1983): that such positional goods are empirically of relatively limited importance; that the notion of 'positionality' is unnecessary and can be replaced by that of 'coerced competition'; that such social-cum-status factors in consumption were as important in the earlier periods of capitalist development; that technological changes in modern capitalism (especially of consumer durables) have considerably reduced the time spent on domestic labour and their purchase is not therefore merely to be viewed as resulting from positional competition; and that Hirsch over-emphasizes both the degree to which capitalism's 'moral legacy' is 'pre-capitalist' and the degree to which it has collapsed in the postwar period.

There are more general difficulties with this form of action-based analysis; in particular insufficient attention is paid to how modern societies are organized through the 'anatomy' of their basic interdependent structures (cf. Urry, 1981). Emphasis is placed upon the lack of moral restraint which then supposedly permits widespread distributional competition between individual actors. In any event, the renewed prominence of rational-choice theories in the social sciences has forced us to consider a social which is secondary and derivative because group cohesion is re-conceived in terms of individual rationality. Next, we will consider game-theoretic Marxism, in which certain notions from rational choice theory are applied to the actions of social *classes* and to the overall structuring of different kinds of society.

Class Action and Game-Theoretic Marxism

John Roemer (see 1981, 1982a, 1982b) aims to establish clear and distinct 'micro-foundations' for social science and especially for Marxist social science. For Roemer (1982a, p. 514), 'methodological individualism is a deductive method; it attempts to deduce historical observations from basic postulates on individual behaviour that are sufficiently fundamental to be considered self-evident'. It is Roemer who is the most 'fundamentalist' of the theoretic Marxists in as much as he devotes the least attention to conditions which encourage a co-operative solution to games. Roemer (1981, p. 7) sees the basic task of Marxist economics to be the derivation of 'the aggregate behaviour of an economy as a consequence of individuals who are postulated to behave in some specific way'. He attempts to demonstrate that such a methodological individualist analysis would enable the explanation of complex social processes and institutional arrangements which functional analysis cannot explain.

To illustrate his approach we note Roemer's analyses of the concept of 'exploitation'. He concentrates first on the 'Class Exploitation Correspondence Principle' and begins with three postulates: (1) that individuals engage in optimizing behaviour; (2) that there exist specific institutional arrangements, particularly different markets; and (3) that there is a differential distribution of wealth or capital stocks. Initially he considers petty commodity production, in which there are commodity and capital markets but not labour markets. He argues that those with superior stocks of capital goods exploit those with lesser stocks (in effect through markets) because the latter have to devote more labour time to subsistence than do the former. He then introduces the market for labour into analysis and argues, with the assumption of labour-minimizing optimization, that exploitation exists because of the unequal labour times required to obtain subsistence. As a consequence, producers 'optimising' against a wealth [in capital goods] constraint, place themselves in one of [five] social classes' (Roemer, 1982b, p. 261). Roemer subsequently introduces additional institutional arrangements such as credit markets and capital accumulation. Exploitation, he maintains, is a question of the relationship between, on the one hand, the labour time embodied in bundles of goods that the producer can purchase with the revenues obtained and, on the other hand, the actual labour time worked by the producer.

Roemer, secondly, elaborates the notion of exploitation in more conventionally game-theoretic terms. By definition, 'a group [can] be conceived of as exploited if it has some *conditionally feasible alternative* under which its members would be better off'; that is 'if a coalition [in a game played by coalitions of agents in the economy] can do better for its members by "withdrawing" [from the economy], then it is exploited' (Roemer, 1982b, p. 276; original emphasis). In feudalism this withdrawal would be by serfs with their own private assets; in capitalism by the coalition of wage-earning producers with their per capita share of society's alienable productive assets. In socialism a class would be exploited if members were better off through withdrawal with their per capita share of society's 'inalienable assets' (that is, skill, qualifications).

Jon Elster has criticized Roemer's second, game-theoretic, version of exploitation for its dependence on counterfactual statements (that is only in terms of hypothetical alternatives). Exploitation for Elster (1982) is above all causal and interactional. He argues in particular for the importance of two basic premises of rational choice theory: (1) that structural constraints do not completely determine the actions individuals take; and (2) that within the feasible set of actions compatible with the constraints, and possessed with a given 'preference structure', an individual will choose those that he or she believes will bring the best results. Analysis of such rational choices involves game theory, particularly because of the necessity to investigate the *interdependence of decisions*. Game theory has a particular contribution to make to Marxist social science, 'because classes crystallize into collective actors that confront each other over the distribution of income and power, as well as over the nature of property relations; and as there are also strategic relations between the members of a given class, game theory is needed to explain these complex interdependencies' (Elster, 1982, p. 464; and see 1983, p. 77).

In *Logic and Society*, following his analysis of various kinds of social contradiction, Elster (1978, pp. 134–50) argues that appropriate collective action is likely to develop and to be more successful: (1) the more that actors *perceive* that there is some kind of contradiction characterizing the society within which they are implicated; (2) the lower the 'communicational distance' between the members; (3) the less the rate of *turnover* in group membership; and (4) the greater the degree to which contradictions are reversible. More specifically, Elster argues that, through continued interaction, workers in particular become both concerned and informed about each other. Concern for others changes the ranking of preferences, and information about others enables actors to realize the solution of the ensuing game. This is termed the 'assurance game' where individuals choose 'universal co-operation' over the free-rider outcome. However, this solution rests upon perfect information – where the information is poor workers will prefer 'universal egoism' (a free-rider outcome) rather than one in which they may all be 'suckers'. Leadership of political groups or trade unions is important in communicating such information and making possible the 'conditional altruism' of the assurance game (Elster, 1982, pp. 469–70).

Crucial in this context, however, is the periodization of the rationality. In *Logic and Society* Elster (1978, ch. 5) had analysed two types of contradictions in social action, 'counterfinality' and 'suboptimality'. In a debate with Charles Taylor (1980), he argues that, in pre-modern societies, the main contradiction is 'counterfinality', which 'occurs because every actor assumes that he is working within a thing-like environment which in reality is made up of (or the result of the actions of) other intentional actors' (Elster, 1980, p. 216). This means that action will have unanticipated, often 'tragic', consequences. In an intermediate stage agents see that others respond to their environment and adapt to their action to take advantage of this perception. In a third stage agents come to realize that others are reasoning about the reasoning of other agents as well as about their reasoning. This is the beginning of game-theoretic or strategic action where the 'dominant form of social contradiction' is 'suboptimality' (Elster, 1980, p. 218), best illustrated in the unhappy, unanticipated consequences which occur in the prisoner's dilemma game. A fourth stage of the development of rational action would also be game-theoretic and is characterized by overcoming the contradiction of 'suboptimality'. In it the shared knowledge of the shared preferences of others would lead individuals to the assurance game's preference of universal co-operation over the free-rider solution and universal egoism.

There are a number of difficulties in Elster's particularly insightful discussion of the nature of human action. First, as Stinchcombe (1980) argues, solutions to games are often provided by social structures themselves. In the case of both erotic love and the decision about whether or not to work, social structural pressures external to the game itself foster 'co-operative' solutions. The dilemmas of action are solved without ever being faced. Secondly, Stinchcombe also argues that there may be general mechanisms in social life, analogous to 'evolutionary mechanisms' in biology, which can account for 'functional adaptation'. He describes this as a 'Deweyan pragmatist consciousness [which] is exactly what is required to complete the functionalist causal loop' (Stinchcombe, 1980, p. 192). Such a consciousness arises when social structural pressures create a state of disequilibrium in individuals. This leads to an awareness of problems and as a result individuals gradually transform the functional element towards that appropriate to re-establish equilibrium. In other words, Stinchcombe incorporates the analysis of the social – 'learning and consciousness' – as well as the irreversibility of time, into his critique of the static and unreflective presuppositions of the agent in game-theory.

A third problem is that Elster defines class consciousness operationally as the capacity of a class to overcome the free-rider problem. This would translate empirically into the incorrect proposition that the Swedish and Austrian working classes are the most class conscious in the West, and French the least class conscious. What Elster ignores are the diverse ideological conditions that cannot be simply reduced to whether the members of different classes are or are not in close interaction with one another. In the United States, for example, the widespread existence of individualistic ideologies appears to lower union membership and to maximize prisoner's dilemma preference structures by comparison with the United Kingdom or Italy. Finally, Elster views classes as essentially comprised of individual actors who may or may not engage in collective action. Missing from his analysis is an examination of classes as comprising sets of 'resources, capacities, and powers' which may be realized within specific conjunctures. Analyses of resources, capacities and powers are crucially relevant to assessing whether a particular class can be collectively organized, and to the outcomes of such organization, both for the class in question and for other social forces within that society (Lash and Urry, 1984).

This focus on agency can also be seen in Offe and Wiesenthal's (1980) analysis of the different forms taken by labour and by capital when they organize collectively. The crucial feature of labour is its *individuality*; it is atomized and divided by competition. Labour cannot merge, merely associate. Also, because of the indissoluble links between labourers and their labour-power, associations of labour must organize a wider spectrum of the needs of labour. Capital, by contrast, is united and organized to maximize profits, this being a matter which can generally be left to decisions by technical experts. And at the same time, labour has to concern itself with the well-being of capital far more systematically than capital has to concern itself with the conditions of labour. Capital, moreover, possesses three forms of organization – the firm itself, informal co-operation between firms, and the employers' association – whereas labour has merely one. In any conflict between the two capital would seem certain to win since their collective action involves far fewer individuals, they are more united, and they possess clearer goals and greater resources.

Organizations of labour rest upon the 'willingness to act', but those of capital on the 'willingness to pay'. For the latter there is no problem involved in maximizing size; for the former this generates profound dilemmas. This is partly because an increase in size will probably produce a greater degree of bureaucratization, and it will undermine labour's ability to mobilize its power to act. It is also because an increase in size will increase the heterogeneity of occupations and interests represented, and hence will make it more difficult to establish the collective identity (the 'dialogue') necessary for widespread collective action. The larger the organization, the more heterogeneous are the interests that have to be reconciled – not only concerning maximization of members' wages, but also ensuring security of employment, controlling the work process in some ways, and working and living in pleasant conditions. Unlike organizations of capital, which can create and maintain the integration of their membership in a one-dimensional 'monological' manner, organizations of labour are involved in a complex and contradictory process of expressing/forming/sustaining a common identity. The organization in part has to function 'dialogically', whereby the activity and views of the membership have to be expressed and developed through dialogue. Offe and Wiesenthal argue that the organizations of capital are 'monological', but those of labour have to be both 'monological' and 'dialogical'. Offe and Wiesenthal suggest that in recent decades the monological has increasingly come to replace the dialogical as the predominant form of organization of labour. The free-rider issue is secondary; after a certain organizational size is reached, it is not increased membership, but the disappearance of the dialogical, which is the main problem.

This highly instructive argument suffers from certain difficulties (cf. Abercrombie and Urry, 1983, ch. 8). First, it is not clear what the relationship is between the dialogical and the development of collective action and radicalism of either an industrial or a political sort (Lash, 1984b, ch. 8). Second, it is difficult to explain the situation in the United States where there is low union density combined with overwhelmingly monological organizations of labour. It would seem necessary to consider the profoundly important development of the collective action of other classes, particularly the service class, whose partially realized causal powers can be seen in the movement for 'scientific management', the enormous expansion of college education, and the development of a status based on educational credentials. These have severely weakened the American working class and produced the shift towards monological forms at lower levels of organizational membership. Third, there are important properties of language and society which cannot be easily expressed as qualities or descriptions of either individual or collective agents. Particularly important here is the way that language provides 'cultural resources' which do not simply constrain actions but which *permit* various kinds of action to be organized and sustained. In the next section we will consider some recent literature on language and action developed from within a tradition in which the focus on the supposed 'rationality' of actions is seen as itself something to be transcended.

Sensual-Aesthetic Forms of Agency

We shall show now that a further major attack on the significance of the social, particularly of its structuration, has been developed by a number of influential French writers, some of whom are generally thought of as 'structuralists'. Let us turn first to Jacques Lacan who, according to conventional wisdom, offers a 'culturalist' rather than a 'naturalist' interpretation of Freud. It is possible, however, to see Lacan's 'structuralism' as an anti-structuralism and his 'culturalism' as a naturalism. In his capacity as anti-structuralist and naturalist, Lacan has participated in the theoretical war of attrition which promises the dissolution of the social.

Lacan is said to be a structuralist in as much as he views 'the subject' as being constituted through structure. This proposition, however, makes little sense unless we first ask what is meant by subject and structure (cf. Coward and Ellis, 1977). On the first point, it is clear that the subject for Lacan is Freud's ego, and those who have equated Lacan's 'subject' with agency or the social actor have badly misconstrued Lacan's theoretical framework. Lacanian theory has its basis in the critique of psychoanalytical ego theory, and it is precisely against those who would begin to equate the ego with agency that Lacan wants to argue. Ego psychologists have understood psychic normality in terms of the healthy ego, which – through a set of varied resources, including the ego's unconscious defence mechanisms – has the environment and the id well under control. Lacan deplores any view in which the ego acts as legislator and monitor to the unconscious; he prescribes instead a notion of agency, in which the derivative nature of the ego is understood and the creative play of the unconscious is given much greater scope (Lacan, 1984).

Now let us consider structure. Those who would insist that Lacan is a structuralist would point to the Saussurean influence in his work. Clearly the term 'structuralist' is of little use apart from Saussure's conception whereby *langue*, or the differential relationships between signifiers in a language, constitute meaning, concepts and the subject. What Lacan does, however, is to subvert Saussure and relocate *langue* – which more orthodox structuralists such as Barthes (and perhaps Saussure) understood as external and constraining in much the sense of Durkheim's *conscience collective* – in agency itself. This partly anti-structuralist rendering of Lacan is all the more plausible if we contrast his theoretical project with Durkheim's.

For Durkheim the *conscience collective* in modernity was to ground a rational-moral version of individualism, which was constructed as a barrier against the dark irrational forces of anomie. Lacan, by contrast, attempts to rescue these forces in the unconscious from the tyranny of a structurally constituted rational-moral ego.

The same can be said, it now follows, in regard to Lacan's putative culturalism. Culture for Lacan is not situated in a Durkheimian framework, or in a late Freudian ego-based concept like 'civilization'. Indeed, if culture must be understood in terms of an instrumental or a rational-moral ego, then Lacan is a naturalist. Or, at best, he is a culturalist only to the extent that he relocates the cultural in the natural (Mitchell, 1982; Safonan, 1968). In this sense, then, Lacan's work has been part and parcel of the theoretical offensive against the social. He has relocated a number of structural entities – language, culture, the unconscious itself – into a reconceived theory of agency, one which pits an ethics of the aesthetic and the sensual against the tyranny of a structurally-posited rational ego.

However, for social theorists such as Gilles Deleuze and Jean-Francois Lyotard, Lacan has only gone halfway in liberating agency from the oppressive rationality of the social (Deleuze and Guattari, 1977; Lyotard, 1980b). The problem for these writers is that Lacan, in his battles against the instrumentally rational individual (which in turn was constituted through social structures while aided and abetted by orthodox psychoanalytic notions), had brought in structure again, so to speak, through the back door. Lacan had done so, Deleuze and Guattari suggested, through the introduction of the structures of language and the family into the unconscious and hence into agency itself. For these critics, grounding the ego in a linguistically structured unconscious was not at issue; the problem was more that Lacan saw the structural characteristics of the family as determinants of how language would in fact codify the unconscious. For Lacan, 'desire' determined how language would impart form to the unconscious. 'Desire' in this context was understood along the lines of Freud's concept of 'wish'; desire was the never-to-be-satisfied Oedipal longing to have the mother and to be the object of the mother's desire, the phallus. The point here, proclaimed Deleuze and Guattari, is not just that Lacan's conceptions reinforced phallocentric and normalized conceptions of the family; it is also that such notions again opened the door to domination through the structured rationality of capitalist society. Lacan, in his critique of ego-psychology, had perhaps freed the subject from direct subjugation – through the conscious mind – from the instrumental rationality bequeathed by a commodity society. But his hierarchical and normalizing notions of desire, and hence the coding of libidinal impulses, allowed capitalist domination to be re-introduced through the unconscious itself (cf. Deleuze and Guattari, 1977).

For Deleuze and Guattari, Lacan's recasting of agency, in which language and the family are transplanted from the social into the unconscious, was not radical enough. Structure too must be expelled, along with the family and language. Desire must be reconceptualized, not as 'wish', but as Freudian libido. Deleuze and Guattari, however, do not completely reject the social. In an attempt to combine Marx and Nietzsche, desire was for them coded by each social formation. In pre-capitalist societies libido was over-coded by a set of symbolisms; capitalism was a result of decodification, the only structuration of desire now being through the commodity form; post-capitalist society would bring the end of codification altogether.

For Lyotard neither Deleuze and Guattari, nor anyone else, has gone far enough. Lyotard wants to do away with structure, with the social altogether; his project is best indicated in the title of his book *Dérive à partir de Marx et Freud* (*Casting Adrift from Marx and Freud*). In any consistent reading of Freud the whole of the psychic apparatus is not only grounded in the id, but is produced or constituted through libido. In what Lyotard has called a 'libidinal metaphysics', not only are our psyches built through libido, but paintings, music, economic processes and social and political institutions are also made of congealed libido. The only difference between more repressive and less repressive institutions, or between classical and post-modernist works of art, is that in each of the former cases libido is to a greater extent turned against itself (Lyotard, 1973; 1980a).

Desire appeared to be everywhere and structure nowhere, having been, it seemed, fully expelled even from agency, in social-theoretical France of the middle 1970s. The only possibility of a further radicalization of agency would be to argue that desire itself was integral to structure. This indeed was part of Foucault's (1980a, pp. 65 ff.) project in the *History of Sexuality*, in which desire was understood as part of discourse and part and parcel of modernity's structures of domination and power. His epistemological writings aside, Foucault was the unsurpassed purveyor of an anti-structuralist ethics, capable of finding a constraining side to any potentially liberating concept. Foucault joined the contemporaneous Roland Barthes in a rejection of desire for a notion of agency, a concept of the body which was to be understood purely in terms of pleasure, or in Foucault's case of an oriental-type *ars erotica* which was counterposed to any *scientia sexualis* (Barthes, 1976; Foucault, 1980a).

We have thus elucidated some qualitative changes in important bodies of contemporary French social theory in which structure and the social have been progressively displaced by agency. This point applies not only to the 'poststructuralists' – to Deleuze, Guattari, Lyotard and Foucault, whose influence has been primarily Nietzschean – but also to the Saussurean 'structuralists', to Lacan, as we saw above, to Barthes and to Derrida. Such structuralism had begun in the early and middle 1960s in France in the context of an anti-rationalist *ambiance*, in which younger thinkers were writing against the Hegelianism, the rationalist Marxism and the existentialism of their teachers (cf. Descombes, 1980). What the structuralists were arguing for was not the apotheosis of structure, but rather the opposition of the 'play of the signifier', of free-flowing, aesthetic and sensual notions of subjectivity, against the holistic and totalizing rationalisms of the previous generation.

Conclusions

We have thus considered three different attempts to re-emphasize the role and importance of agency within contemporary social theory. One major consequence of this re-emphasis has been the decline of, and in some instances the elimination of, a distinct notion of the social from these 'sociological theories'. These developments have so far been more significant in Europe than in North America. This is partly because structural deterministic theories were previously more influential in Western Europe and this has, in a sense, produced a number of opposites. In the United States sociological theory has remained more firmly tied to the classic divisions of 'structure' and 'action', 'conflict' and 'consensus', 'meaning' and 'exchange'. In Europe these divisions, and indeed Parsons's attempts to develop a transcending grand theory, were never influential (except in West Germany). 'Sociological theory' was never bifurcated as a project in Europe as it has been in the United States.

Furthermore, we think that a complex of social conditions have particularly affected some countries in Western Europe and have contributed to the theoretical dissolution of the all-pervasive 'social'. These developments in sociological theory discussed above are at least connected with what we term the 'disorganization' of contemporary capitalist relations (see Lash and Urry, 1985; Offe, 1985). We think that with the increasingly post-industrial structuring of contemporary capitalism, the seemingly never-ending round of economic and legitimation crises, theories of structure have lost some of their plausibility. This is particularly the case in those societies which have most dramatically 'disorganized' in recent years, in France, Germany, the Low Countries, United Kingdom, and Scandinavia to a lesser extent. The United States has been 'disorganized' for over a generation or two and action theories have always enjoyed considerable popularity.

Nevertheless in both Europe and North America, theories of an omnipotent 'structure' no longer appear as credible to either the sociological right or left. In the case of the right, for those who have noted a clear absence of anything like a healthily functioning totality, structural-functionalism has lost meaning and explanatory value. Thus, the neo-conservative writers around *Commentary* have turned to considerations of collective actors in their 'overload' theory, in which the state is, so to speak, 'overloaded' with the demands of a multiplicity of organized groups (see Brittan, 1975 and above). Similarly, cultural conservatives such as Christopher Lasch and Daniel Bell have turned their theoretical ammunition against agency conceived as narcissism, desire, or aesthetic modernism (Bell, 1976; Lasch, 1983).

On the left as well, a theoretical crisis has ensued, this time in conjunction with the decline in the size and power of the industrial working class and the concomitant rise of the social movements in 'disorganized capitalism' (Lash and Urry, 1985). Here the vision of a social, structured through the contradiction of capital and labour, has been irreparably fragmented, and a structural Marxism rendered less plausible, while a new Marxism of collective action has arisen. Many theorists of the left have also begun to reformulate the class-versus-class contradiction as bureaucratic and repressive rationality versus communicative and ecological-aesthetic forms of individual and collective agency. Thus emerges the meaningfulness to many on the left of the 'post-Marxism' of Frankfurt critical theory and French social theory. Although it is too soon for more than speculation, the disorganization of capitalism and the theoretical dissolution of the social appear – in some sort of elective affinity – to be proceeding apace hand in hand.

This decline of structural-functionalism, on the one hand, and structural Marxism, on the other, corresponds to what Richard Rorty has called a dissolution of 'metanarratives'. This destruction of the totalizing, structurally-determinist metanarratives has opened up a theoretical space for the reconstruction of the theory, or theories, of action. In this context, there are two choices available to social-action theorists. Either they can, as Parsons did in 1937 and Habermas has re-iterated in 1981, through the exegesis and interpretation of the 'classical' sociological metanarratives, attempt to produce a new, totalizing theory of action. Or they can (for example, Giddens, 1979), no less ambitiously, but without totalizing pretensions or expectations, draw parasitically, as it were, on a heterogeneous variety of neighbouring (such as political theory, philosophy, French avant-garde theory) discourses in order to recast our understanding of social action. In Europe, in any event, an increasing number of theorists are taking the latter tack and it is these which we have analysed here.

PART IV

PRACTICE AND THE RECONSTRUCTION OF SOCIOLOGICAL THEORY

8

Actors and Social Relations

Barry Hindess

> ... people of my generation were brought up on these two
> forms of analysis, one in terms of the constituent subject, the
> other in terms of the economic in the last instance, ideology
> and the play of superstructures and infrastructures. (Foucault,
> 1980b, p. 116)

The picture presented here by Foucault's interviewers may be a little
overdrawn; these were not the only forms of social analysis on offer,
although they may have been the most distinctive and even, in some
respects, the most rigorous. But there can be no doubt that modern social
thought has been plagued by the varieties of theoretical humanism and
structuralism. This essay explores some of the consequences of
abandoning them. Foucault's own work is not without problems,[1] but he
is surely correct in insisting on the need to get away from these forms of
analysis. The first insists that social life is to be understood in terms of the
constitutive actions of human individuals. The second analyses social life
in terms of the functioning of social wholes (totalities) in which necessary
effects are seen as produced by the action of the structure. The tensions
between these positions appear in recurrent disputes about the
relationship between individual and society, for example, in the charge
that Parsonian functionalism operates with an 'oversocialized' conception
of man. Each side in these disputes is able to trade off the obvious
weaknesses of the other, the difficulty of denying that individuals do
indeed make choices and act upon them on the one hand, and the merely
gestural character of attempts to account for structural features of social
life as the products of those decisions on the other.

But, for all the obvious opposition between these positions there is also
a certain complicity between them. In one the human individual is a
creative subject, freely constituting actions and social relations. In the
other the human individual is literally the subject of (that is, subjected to)

the system of social relations in which 'it' internalizes its part and subsequently acts it out. What is shared here is a conception of the human subject as characterized by essential attributes of will and subjectivity; as a condition of its creative activity in the one case and of its subjection to its position in the structure in the other.[2] Both are reductionist in the sense that they propose to reduce social conditions of diverse kinds to others that are supposed to be more basic either to structural conditions or to creative actions of individuals. These reductionisms and the perpetual disputes between them allow their protagonists to avoid posing serious theoretical and political questions.

I have argued elsewhere against both structuralism and theoretical humanism (Cutler *et al.*, 1977, 1978; Hindess, 1977). Rather than repeat those arguments here I suggest an alternative approach to social theory, neither structuralist nor humanist, and consider some of its implications for the role of theoretical work in political calculation. What is involved here is a radical anti-reductionism according to which social phenomena are always dependent on definite and specifiable conditions of diverse kinds. These conditions include the decisions and actions of actors and social conditions that are clearly external to any individual and which are not themselves reducible to any general principle of explanation.

In contrast to any thoroughgoing structuralism it is important to recognize that actors do indeed reach decisions and act on them, that their actions are in part a consequence of their decisions. Decisions themselves are reached through processes that are internal to the actor in question, that is, they are not reducible to the expression of the actor's position within a system of social relations. Some version of this proposition is shared by most contributions to this volume, but I shall depart from at least some of their arguments in several important respects. In particular, I shall argue first that there are actors other than human individuals and, secondly, that actors' decisions and actions depend on conditions that are social in the sense of being external to the actor concerned. It follows that social relations cannot be reduced to the creative activity of those engaged in them, and in particular that they cannot be reduced to the constitutive acts of human individuals. The creative human individual is not the essential starting point for social analysis. But my argument is equally opposed to those who regard the concept of the social system as a functioning whole as providing the essential starting point. For example, many versions of Marxism regard capitalist society as a social totality essentially structured by the pattern of class relations given in the dominant mode of production. The pattern of class relations defines the basic social forces at work in the society and the changes that can be achieved within it. The objective structure of society, therefore, provides the essential starting point for any serious political analysis. I argue on the contrary that there is no essential structure that determines what politics, and therefore political analysis, must be about. In any given society there are definite connections between its various component parts, but no overall determining structure.

After considering concepts of actor and social structure, this essay concludes by discussing some of the implications of these arguments for the place of political concerns and objectives in relation to social theory and social analysis. What is important as the starting point of analysis depends on its objectives; it is not given in the essential structure of society. In so far as those objectives are political, the way social relations are analysed will be informed by political concerns and objectives.

Social Actors and Human Individuals

This section discusses the concept of actor, arguing that, although the notion is often misused, there are indeed actors other than human individuals, some of whom play a major role in the modern world, and that social life is irreducible to the constitutive action of actors. An actor is a locus of decision and action, where the action is in some sense a consequence of the actor's decisions. This conception may seem formal and abstract, but we shall see that it has far reaching consequences. In particular, reference to an actor always involves some reference to definite means of reaching and formulating decisions, definite means of action, and some links between the two. Human individuals are actors in this sense, but they are clearly not the only entities that reach decisions and act accordingly. Capitalist enterprises, state agencies, political parties and church organizations are examples of social actors: they all have means of reaching and formulating decisions and of acting on at least some of them.

In a loose sense of course the claim that there are social actors, other than human individuals, appears to be widely accepted. But the wide acceptance involves a heavy theoretical cost. The concept of social actor has to be defended against two kinds of abuse; against, on the one hand, its extension to cover entities that are actors in only the most allegorical of senses, and, on the other, the claim that social actors are themselves reducible to human individuals. Let us consider these abuses in turn. An actor is something that formulates decisions and acts on them, and I have just given several examples of actors other than human individuals. Problems arise when the concept of actor is extended to include collectivities that have no identifiable means of formulating decisions, let alone of acting on them. In contrast to capitalist enterprises which do have definite means of reaching and formulating decisions and of acting on many of them, 'classes' and 'societies' clearly do not. Reference to classes as actors is either allegorical or else, at best, a shorthand way of referring to a set of specific actors (human individuals, various groups and organizations) whose actions are thought to be identifiable with the interests of particular classes. Much Marxist and Weberian discussion slides uneasily between these usages. The problematic effects of treating classes as actors can be seen most clearly in Marxist and other influential forms of political analysis (Cutler *et al.*, 1977, 1978; Hindess, 1983). As for societies, their treatment as actors is, if anything, even more widespread. Sometimes the usage is merely colloquial, as when government is treated as speaking for the 'nation' or 'society' it governs. Such cases need not detain us here. Other cases are more serious. For example, Talcott Parsons (1964) treats social systems as actors, allocating the decision-making role to the functional sub-systems – primarily to the polity. This is not the place to discuss Parsons's work in any detail. For present purposes it is sufficient to notice that his treatment of social systems as actors slides between allegory and shorthand in much the same way as many Marxist treatments of class. In so far as 'societal' decisions can be identified, they are formulated by specific actors (governments and state agencies) or they are not formulated at all. What is at stake in this latter is an influential way of treating some state of affairs as the result of society's decision. In his powerful argument against the individualism of rational choice arguments, Levi goes so far as to suggest that

> It is not incoherent to regard a society that allocates commodity bundles through a market mechanism as an agent. The market mechanism in operation provides a procedure whereby the society makes certain kinds of 'social choice' ... Of course many decisions are involved in the allocation of goods in a market economy, but at no point does 'society' formulate a decision in favour of precisely that allocation and no other. (Levi, 1982, p. 236)

There are indeed actors other than human individuals, but classes and societies are not among them. This restriction of the concept of actor to things that formulate decisions and act on them is important for two reasons. First, actors' decisions are an important part of the explanation of their actions. To extend that category of actor to collectivities that have no means of formulating decisions, and then to treat what happens as resulting from their decision (as in the example above), is therefore to obscure the social processes resulting in those conditions. Secondly, only those who take decisions and act on them can be held responsible, and the assignment of responsibility plays an important part in the analysis of social conditions and of what can be done to change them. Arguments that assign responsibility to fictitious actors are politically misleading. To blame 'society' for some state of affairs may be a way of suggesting that changes are desirable, but tells us nothing about how they may be brought about.

The second error, of treating social actors as reducible to human individuals, is an example of the more general project of methodological individualism. I have suggested a certain complicity between structuralism and theoretical humanism in a conception of the human subject. In this respect a methodological individualism may be compatible both with theoretical humanism and with structuralism. For example, rational choice models in politics and economics commonly treat actors' forms of thought as given by the social category to which they belong – as entrepreneurs, consumers, voters, political leaders, or whatever. Here a methodological individualism is combined with the structural determination of actors' forms of thought (Hindess, 1984). Or again, many forms of Marxist class analysis and non-Marxist studies of political behaviour regard individuals as possessing interests that are given as a consequence of their membership of particular social categories. Here, too, the effect of taking actors' decisions seriously is to show that the individualistic project cannot be sustained.

The reaching of decisions involves the deployment of some discursive means whereby objectives, arguments and analyses are formulated, and in which the actor is located in relation to those objectives and decisions. To say that actors *deploy* discursive means of formulating objectives and reaching decisions in relation to them is to say that their objectives and decisions depend on how those discursive means are deployed. They are not determined by any situational logic as a function of actors' location within a set of social relations, of their class position, education, sex, or whatever. Actors do not have given ends, interests or objectives.

But to say that actors deploy *discursive means* is also to raise serious questions of the discursive means employed by or available to actors. These questions are obscured by theories that treat rationality as a property of the actor. Instrumental rationality, where it appears, is a property of the decisions that actors formulate, and therefore of the discursive conditions in which those decisions are reached. It is not an intrinsic feature of the actor *qua* actor. Many readers will no doubt demur at this point; is not the presumption of a common human rationality a precondition of communication and understanding, of the interpretation of cultures (our own and others'), and indeed of the very possibility of human social existence? Underneath our cultural differences do we not share a common humanity?

This is not the place to attempt to disentangle all the many strands of that objection. For present purposes it is sufficient to note that the apparent success of at least some level of communication and understanding across the most diverse cultures does not justify the presumption of a *rationality* that is common to all cultures, and therefore independent of specific discursive conditions.[3] The possibility of communication and understanding certainly requires that some common ground can be found between the communicating parties. It does not follow that the same common ground is there to be found in all cases, still less that there is a universal core consisting in a characteristically human rationality that is exhibited in the way every human actor reaches decisions.

These questions of the discursive means employed by and available to actors are also obscured by theories that derive actors' forms of thought from their structural location. For example, many Marxist and neo-classical economists argue that a process of natural selection operates amongst enterprises, so that the survivors are profit maximizers. In fact it is not difficult to show that several quite distinct modes of economic calculation may be employed by firms operating within a single national economy (Cutler *et al.*, 1978; Winter, 1964, 1971, 1975). There is no uniquely defined mode of economic calculation (profit-maximizing) that is employed by enterprises as a function either of their supposed rationality or of the rigours of the marketplace.

These essentially negative points have important positive implications. If rationality were a property of the actor *qua* actor or if forms of thought were given by the actor's structural location, then there would be no need to inquire further into the conditions necessary for actors' decisions to take the form that they do. They take that form because they are actors, and therefore rational, or because they are actors belonging to the category of entrepreneurs, political leaders, or whatever – and that is all there is to it. To dispute these positions is therefore to raise questions concerning the discursive means employed by or available to actors and questions of the social conditions on which they depend.[4] I say 'employed by or available to' here to guard against the all too convenient assumption that actors have only one means of formulating objectives and assessing their situation. In many contexts, for example, election campaigns or disputes over the unionization of companies in the United States, the forms of discourse available to actors allow the formulation of a variety of distinct objectives and assessments – and it is this that provides the scope for persuasion, propaganda and other political work aimed at changing actors' assessments. If the decisions formulated by actors depend on conditions which are not inherent features of the actors themselves, then social life is not reducible to the constitutive behaviour of actors. Once that is admitted in the case of human actors, there can be no reason for supposing (like Weber) that, in general, social actors are reducible to the constitutive acts of human individuals.

Finally, although I have concentrated here on the importance of discursive means of reaching and formulating decisions in showing that social life is irreducible to the constitutive behaviour of actors, similar points could be made by reference to the means of action. It is trivially true, for example, that the action of social actors involves the actions of others. Human individuals may not be the constitutive subjects of social life, but they are the only actors whose actions do not invariably involve the actions of others. Nevertheless, many of the most significant kinds of action clearly depend on conditions that are external to the acting individual. For example, the actions of capitalist employers depend on certain legal rights over the disposition of the property of the enterprise and also over what employees may be required to do or not to do. They may also depend on the use of various control techniques involving hierarchical chains of command and supervision, the collection of information, and so on. Here the means of action that crucially distinguish the position of the capitalist (whether human individual or joint-stock company) from that of an employee depend precisely on their differential location within several intersecting sets of social relations.

Social Structure

The discussion this far has left open the content of 'social', as it appears in concepts of 'social relations' and 'social structure'. It has indicated ways in which decisions and actions depend on conditions that are 'social' in the minimal sense of being external to the actors concerned. So far, perhaps, so good. But more should be said about the analysis of social conditions. My coauthors and I have argued elsewhere against the analysis of society as a totality governed by necessary structural requirements, whether these be conceived in terms of laws of motion deriving from the domination of a particular mode of production, as in many forms of Marxism, or in terms of functional prerequisites resulting from systemic exigencies and the domination of central values (Cutler *et al.*, 1977, 1978; Hindess and Hirst, 1977). Rather, social phenomena should be analysed in terms of their specific conditions of existence without any presumption that those conditions in turn derive from overall structural requirements. To describe a particular society as capitalist is not to say that it is an integrated whole or that its capitalist character yields necessary effects. For example, capitalist relations of production require that certain conditions of existence be met by legal and cultural relations and exchanges. They also require definite means and conditions of production, actors capable of occupying positions of control and subordination in relation to those means of production, and so on. But there can be no warrant for assuming that these diverse conditions of existence will be provided as necessary effects of the capitalist structure of the social formation.

These general arguments against the analysis of society as a totality are reinforced by the conclusions of the previous section. The concept of actor outlined above cannot be reconciled with a concept of society as a functioning whole governed by some unifying principle (dominant mode of production, central values, or whatever) and producing necessary effects as a consequence of its structural exigencies. If actors do indeed act on the basis of decisions, and if those decisions involve complex discursive processes, then there can be no reason to expect actors' decisions to accord with the requirements of society as a functioning whole.

It would be misleading to say that sociologists have entirely failed to recognize this point. Parsons's discussion is particularly clear. The personality system is clearly something that makes decisions, yet Parsons insists that the personality and social systems have distinct, and therefore sometimes incompatible requirements. It follows that providing some reasonable satisfaction for the needs of its personalities must be a perpetual challenge for any social system. The problem with Parsons's argument here, of course, is that his initial identification of the systems of action as *systems* in his sense (as homeostatic and boundary maintaining entities) is itself theoretically arbitrary (Savage, 1981). The concept of actor, as a maker of decisions, poses problems for his concept of social system. But Parsons has no theoretical grounds for translating those theoretical problems into practical problems for functioning social systems, other than dispensing with his concept of social system.

The term 'social', then, should not be understood by reference to the operations of society as a functioning whole. The well-worn sociological demonstration that there are social preconditions of contract does not require us to accept society as an entity operating outside of and above its actors. 'Social' conditions and 'social' structure refer us to a variety of practices and conditions with no overall unifying principle or centre. Precisely what practices or conditions are at issue will vary with the object of inquiry. Consider, for example, the 'social' conditions governing the availability of abortions.[5] What is involved here is the intersection of a variety of medical, legal and bureaucratic practices, and policies of governments and other agencies concerning the regulation of 'moral' practices, public health and nutrition, the specification of certain medical categories in law, the use of statistical population profiles, and so on. 'Social' conditions in this case refer not to the functional exigencies of society, but rather to the complex intersection of a variety of specific practices, policies and actors. The point here has general application: 'social' is a shorthand way of referring to the intersections of consequences of specific practices and the conditions those practices sustain (or undermine).

We are concerned then with 'social' conditions as they relate to the decisions and actions of particular actors, and with the interconnection within those 'social' conditions themselves. Decision and action take place under definite conditions and face definite obstacles, some of which involve the practices of other actors. We are concerned with conceptualizing the sites of decision and action (the conditions in which they take place and the obstacles they confront) and the relationships between different sites. Since there is no common essence to the 'social' and no overarching social totality, it follows that very little can be said about the characteristics of sites in general and the connections between them. But it is possible to make a few points by way of illustration.

I have already suggested some of the ways in which decision and action depend on the deployment of particular discourses and means of action, and therefore on their availability to the actors in question. Precisely what means are available may vary not only from site to site, but also according to the actor's location. Foucault's discussion of medical discourse shows how the availability of discourses may be restricted to the occupants of particular positions within medical institutions (Foucault, 1973). For another example consider how the development of specialist managerial techniques has affected the differential availability of decision-making resources and means of acting on them within large organizations. At the other extreme, there are discursive and other resources so widely available across a variety of sites that they may be regarded as characteristic of particular societies or cultures. Consider the effects of near-universal literacy and the availability of telephones, duplicating and photocopying facilities within the more advanced societies. Or again, in his more recent work, Foucault proposes to analyse relations of power in specific sites in relation to general technologies (institutionalized mechanisms for the operation of power) and strategies (forms of analysing conditions, identifying objectives and means of action which together constitute the world as a field of instrumental action).[6]

As for relations between sites, the most obvious relations concern the way decisions taken in one site can affect, and may be intended to affect, decisions and actions in others. Legislation and judicial decisions, for example, can affect the conditions of action for management and unions across a range of enterprises. A different set of examples would be generalized social discourses and organizational techniques which are or may be employed by actors at a variety of sites: discourses of class or worker solidarity, in which particular conflicts may be represented as parts of a wider struggle, techniques of picketing and other forms of collective action. Such general discourses and means of action can be an important feature of the mobilization of support in particular sites of conflict, and perhaps of generalizing particular conflicts into other arenas

– for example, sympathy strikes and secondary picketing. General social discourses provide ample scope for dispute and interpretation and they frequently cut across other widely available discourses. During the 1984–5 mineworkers' strike in Britain, appeals to internal union democracy cut across the appeal of mineworker-solidarity, with some groups of miners insisting on a national ballot of all mineworkers before agreeing to participate in strike action. In this example, the specific character of the conflict within the union is crucially affected by the availability of distinct and cross-cutting discourses of democracy and solidarity.

A word of warning is in order at this point. Some sites clearly embrace a more general scope than others. Decisions taken at national levels have a different scope and a different range of effects than those taken elsewhere, say, by local governments or employers. It may be tempting to suggest a hierarchical organization, with sites at higher levels incorporating those lower down – for example, a national struggle between capital and labour (more precisely, organizations and individuals that may be said to represent them) incorporating disputes in particular workplace localities. But that would be a serious mistake involving the reintroduction of society-as-totality through a limited number of global sites. Of course, struggles in particular localities may be affected by conditions determined elsewhere at a broader social level, and we have seen that there are all kinds of ways in which the discourses and means of action at particular sites may relate to broader social conditions. But local sites do not thereby lose their separate existences. Decisions and actions taken within local sites may well be affected by what happens elsewhere, but it does not follow that they are determined. National economic planning decisions certainly affect the conditions in which individual enterprises operate but, as governments know, these decisions do not determine their behaviour.

Conclusions

Where do these arguments leave us? Let me begin with some general comments about the analysis of social life before moving on to their political implications. Some readers will no doubt feel disturbed by my undermining of the apparent intellectual certainties provided, albeit in rather different ways, by the varieties of theoretical humanism and structuralism. If we cast these aside, what have we left? I have argued above that reference to our common humanity does not provide an intellectually defensible foundation for the analysis of social life, but what of the other pole? If society is not a functioning whole, then how is a relatively stable and enduring social life possible? If we cannot posit self-sustaining social totalities, how can we hope to make sense of the incredible complexities of human social interaction? This is one of Parsons's fundamental questions, and the 'obviousness' of his answer lies at the heart of his treatment of the systems of action. Similar questions and answers underlie other treatments of society-as-totality.[7]

My purpose in presenting these questions is only to undermine them. They employ the common rhetorical device of suggesting that the only alternative to the 'obvious' answer is chaos – either in social life itself, or in our attempts to make sense of it. If only things were that simple! Neither social life nor our attempts to analyse it ever start from nothing. To say that there are no essential structures of social life provided by the operations of society as a self-sustaining totality is not to say that there are no relatively pervasive or enduring social conditions. Of course there are conditions in some sites of action that are not difficult to change – the relatively easy access to divorce in most Western societies is an example. Other conditions are more enduring. The general forms of law and property relations characteristic of the modern West are sustained not by some necessity inherent in capitalism as a mode of production but because they are situated in complex networks of intersecting practices and conditions. But to say that actors formulate decisions and act on them and, further, that those decisions are not wholly determined by the social conditions in which they are made, is to say neither that the patterns of social interaction are essentially fragile and unpredictable, nor that actors have carte blanche. Actors make decisions and act accordingly, but they do so on the basis of the discursive means and means of action available to them. To a large extent those means are not a matter of choice. Actors can and sometimes do work to change how they (and others) think, but they cannot adopt entirely new discursive forms quickly or at will. Readers who doubt this are invited to try purging their thinking of the effects of literacy.

As for the analysis of social life, if relatively stable and enduring social conditions do not depend on the self-sustaining activities of an overarching social totality, then there is no reason (certainly no good one) to posit such a totality as a precondition for social analysis. There are relatively enduring connections between political and legal practices and conditions and forms of economic organization in most societies, and there is no need to posit some *necessity* in those conditions as a precondition for analysing them.[8]

Finally, what is the bearing of these arguments on the relations between political concerns and objectives and the analysis of social life? Two sets of issues seem to me important here: one concerns social actors, the other concerns social structure. I have argued that there are important actors in the modern world other than human individuals. That point is unlikely to be disputed, but the next is more contentious: that the decisions and actions of social actors are not reducible to those of human individuals. The significance of that point can be seen if we contrast it with one of the fundamental principles of liberal political philosophy, namely, that human individuals can and should be the ultimate point of reference for decisions about social conditions and objectives. The principle has a considerable influence on social and political thought in the modern West. It appears in most forms of contemporary democratic theory, in the diverse forms of liberalism inspired by Hayek, Rawls and Nozick, in public choice theory in economics, and in most versions of rational choice theory in political analysis. Little remains of that principle if we insist: first that there are actors other than human individuals and, secondly, that many significant social decisions are the decisions of social actors (of governments, trades unions, large corporations, churches) – that is, they are not simply aggregations of the decisions of human individuals. Of course, social actors are not immortal, and many of them could no doubt be dispensed with without any great loss to the rest of us. Nevertheless, it is impossible to conceive of a complex modern society in which social actors of this sort did not play a major role. The problem is that the usefulness of an approach to contemporary politics that admits only human individuals as effective actors must be critically diminished in the face of the manifest significance of social actors in the modern world. Social actors may be subjected to controls and restrictions but in general they cannot be dispensed with. They have concerns and objectives that are not reducible to those of human individuals. For example, capitalist enterprises, trades unions, community organizations and local communities all have an interest in the economic policies of governments. Our political theory must learn to take account of the reality of social actors and their effects.

But, if it is essential to take account of the role of social actors in the modern world, there is another sense in which reference to social actors can function as an obstacle to serious and informed political discussion. This occurs when the concept of actor is extended to aggregates that have no identifiable means of formulating decisions, let alone acting on them – societies, communities, classes, racial or gender categories, bureaucracy, or whatever. Of course, there will always be those who claim to formulate decisions on behalf of such aggregates, but the very diversity of such claims should caution us against identifying any one of them with decisions of the aggregate in question. In fact there are two kinds of problems with the invocation of such social actors. One is that it brings a variety of diverse sites, practices and conditions into a spurious unity. The other is that the unity is treated as an actor, whose decisions and other attributes are supposed to perform an explanatory function; for example, where social or economic conditions are 'explained' as the actions of capital or the ruling class, or of men as a collectivity subordinating women. The invocation of spurious actors in this way may have a polemical function, but it thoroughly obscures both investigation of the conditions and processes responsible for the phenomena in question, and political decisions to what can or should be done about them.

The other problem brings us back to social structure. I have argued that there is no fundamental, overarching structure of society that ties together diverse sites, practices and conditions into a functioning whole. In particular, there is no one set of structural conditions to which serious political analysis must inevitably refer. If there is no fundamental structure, but a rather complex set of connections and interdependencies between sites and practices, then what is important in social analysis from the point of view of political objectives must depend precisely on what those political objectives are. Different political objectives pose different problems for social analysis, and they may lead to divergent accounts of social conditions. This means that a familiar distinction on the left between reform and revolution cannot be sustained. If there is no fundamental structure producing necessary effects, then changes in some social conditions cannot be dismissed as mere reforms, that is, as cosmetic changes leaving that fundamental structure untouched.

Decisions and actions in particular sites always depend on 'social' conditions, but those conditions will be of the most diverse kinds and there is no essential 'social' unity to which they all refer. Another way of making these points would be to affirm the reality of particular sites of decision and action. Conditions in some sites will be affected by what happens elsewhere, and some sites will affect and be affected by a wider range of social conditions than others. But there are no sites in which decision and action are entirely determined in sites that are more general. Decision and action at a national level have a different range of effects from decision and action in local communities or workplaces, but there is no sense in which the one can be entirely subsumed within the other. What happens at each level may have implications for the other, but they nevertheless exist as distinct and separate objects of political concern. Local and limited struggles, if they are important at all, are important in their own right, and not merely as components in something grander.

Notes

I am particularly grateful to Liz Kingdom, Mark Wardell and Gary Wickham for their critical comments on an earlier draft.
1   The critical literature on Foucault in English is generally poor. For critical but not unsympathetic discussions see Cousins and Hussain, forthcoming; Minson, 1980; Wickham, 1983.

2 See Cutler *et al.*, 1977, and the discussion of Althusser's account of the subject in Hirst, 1979.

3 See the careful discussion of the role of language and social relations in the formation of human attributes in Hirst and Woolley, 1982. Arguments for the presumption of a common human rationality have been advanced in several papers by Hollis and Lukes; see, for example, their contributions to Hollis and Lukes, 1982.

4 For examples of such investigations see the discussions of enterprise calculation in Cutler *et al.*, 1978, and of the heterogeneous conditions involved in the development of the medical gaze in Foucault, 1973.

5 This example is taken from Wickham, 1983.

6 See Foucault's 1977, 1980a. His arguments are extremely suggestive, but they are far from being without problems (cf. note 1 above).

7 For a series of exchanges on this subject, see Hindess and Hirst, 1975; Cutler *et al.*, 1977, 1978; and the responses, Ball *et al.*, 1979; Harris, 1978; and then our response in Cutler *et al.*, 1979.

8 See the conclusion to Cutler *et al.*, 1978, and Hindess, 1983, for examples of socialist political analysis that do not depend on such necessities.

9

Human Rights Theory and the Classical Sociological Tradition

Ted R. Vaughan and Gideon Sjoberg

We begin with the premise that there has been a dissolution in the scope and significance of social and moral issues addressed by sociological theory, particularly in American sociology. In the course of this transformation, sociologists, with the exception of scholars such as Wallerstein (1983), have largely abdicated their classical concern with the 'big issues' of the nature and direction of human societies, of the possibilities of enhancing human existence, of the meaning of being human in the fullest and best sense of the term, of large-scale alternatives to social arrangements that undermine the human condition. All such issues inevitably embody normative and moral, as well as empirical, considerations.[1]

Sociological theory has moved steadily towards more formal modes of analysis with an emphasis upon manageable concepts and variables that permit greater precision in testing. This shift has in general substituted greater certitude of knowledge based on concerns of limited scope for significant – albeit imprecise – insights into broader social phenomena. In the process, theoretic attention to the ends and goals of social life has been proscribed in favor of a concentration upon the means by which ongoing social orders can best proceed. Consequently, sociologists have become increasingly involved in the formulation of knowledge directed toward the improvement of the administration of the social order in which the ends are implicitly taken for granted and accepted. Sociological theory and practice have become, as Mills (1961), Gouldner (1970), Habermas (1971, 1974) and others have warned, part of the administrative apparatus and more and more instrumentally and technically oriented.

One of the most significant aspects in the dissolution of theoretical discourse has been a major alteration in the conception of social theory. A new set of criteria must be satisfied for an argument or a set of assertions to be regarded as constituting social theory. Foremost among these criteria is the absolute proscription of moral and political (ideological) considerations from theoretical formulations. Proponents of this now dominant conception of the nature of social theory regard the elimination of these elements as one of its most distinctive features and one of its greatest virtues. Yet, the adoption of this kind of social theory rules out the broader concerns which informed classical sociological discourse.

But contentions that social theorists in fact can maintain ethical- and value-neutrality should not be accepted as given. They tend to represent assertions about what theory ideally should be rather than careful analyses of the nature of social theory and practice. If we are to be concerned with theory – and an understanding of today's social issues – we must begin a reassessment of the nature of social theory itself.

Our central thesis in this context is that all social theories embody some moral orientation. (Conversely, all ethical and moral theories, as MacIntyre, 1981, suggests, contain some kind of social theory.) From this perspective, the dissolution of sociological theory does not represent a condition of natural scientific progress or inevitability, but rather involves a political suppression of moral debate in the interest of a particular moral position embedded in the prevailing conception of the nature of theory. Moral concerns have thus not been eliminated but suppressed; in practice, sociologists accept certain moral perspectives uncritically and weave these into their analysis.

Conceptualizing the Nature of Sociological Theory

In traditional philosophy and social theory, as formulated in somewhat differing ways by Plato and Aristotle, normative and moral considerations took precedence over empirical issues. The nature and conditions of the good society – its ends or goals, its purposes and functions – were the fundamental aims of theoretical inquiry. The knowledge resulting from this sustained discourse provided guidance and criteria for practical living, for the best possible forms of human existence.

As observed by Habermas (1974) and Bellah (1983) this traditional conception of theory and the distinctive forms of inquiry it implied were seriously altered by Hobbes and others in the early stages of Western modernity. Hobbes (1969), urging the application of principles of the emerging natural sciences to human affairs, specifically rejected theoretical discourse on the nature of the good society because the notion of good was not a useful scientific term. In seeking to eliminate the ethical component in social theory, Hobbes asserted (and accepted) the specific ethical ends of survival and security of the individual and then sought to harness scientific inquiry to their attainment. But his implicit contentions, that the ends of society are established in nature itself and that science can contribute to the construction of conditions that facilitate the realization of these ends, have had a profound impact on subsequent generations of social theorists.

Contemporary social theory, in rejecting the classical tradition, had pushed Hobbes's commitment to its extreme. Positivism, especially as reflected in logico-deductive theory as the idealized conception of scientific theory, has justified excluding moral concerns from the public domains of science, and it was argued methodologically that the natural and social sciences are one. From the perspective of positivism, scientific theory admits only statements that are logically true or in principle empirically testable. This is translated into the requirement that theory is comprised only of statements of certain kinds – analytic or synthetic – containing only certain kinds of terms – theoretical or observational. In our reading of the Logical Positivist tradition, the specific usage made of these distinctions has been the primary means for eliminating moral concerns from scientific discourse, since statements containing moral terms are regarded as neither analytic nor synthetic; that is, such statements are not cognitively meaningful, because they are neither logically true nor empirically testable.[2]

Scientific theory takes the form of a logically ordered set of statements permitting the deduction of other statements that can be tested empirically. At the most abstract level, such theory contains statements linking concepts referring to non-observable entities; these statements, in turn, are linked with assertions regarding empirical regularities comprised of concepts referring to observable phenomena; finally, testable hypotheses are derived from the interrelated theoretical statements. Only theoretical statements that have a positive correspondence with empirical observations are accorded the status of scientific knowledge.

Theoretical knowledge, then, is the outcome of the application of these logical and empirical procedures where nature is taken to be the ultimate judge of the truth or falsity of assertions. In terms of these requirements, moral considerations, it is claimed, have been banished from scientific activity. Only the application of a rational and objective set of procedures can reveal to a community of investigators a structure of the social world as it exists.

It is generally conceded in contemporary sociology that, although far from having attained the ideal of the logico-deductive form, scientific theory is nonetheless held as the objective to be attained. But even empiricists who do little to justify, or to carry out, research within the logico-deductive mode of analysis (that is, those who adopt a more 'inductive framework') tend to accept many of the basic tenets of the aforementioned view. Thus, members of the 'Wisconsin school' of empiricism, for example, agree that we cannot be concerned with moral issues, that there can be no scientific knowledge of this realm. The view that sociological theory can be and is value-free links most varieties of sociological theorizing today.[3]

The Dominant Conception of Sociological Theory

If one generally accepts the positivist version of science and scientific theory delineated above as a reasonable approximation of the manner in which contemporary science proceeds, the eradication of moral concerns appears as a plausible ideal. But there are important sociological reasons to suggest that this view contains a serious misconception of the nature of science and thereby misreads the conditions and criteria of social theory. We will argue, furthermore, that the contemporary version of scientific theory errs not only in its assumption of the social, autonomous nature of the scientific process, but that it also conceals a particular kind of moral orientation despite its persistent claim to moral neutrality.

For instance, one central criterion of theoretic acceptability in the logico-deductive format is that of testability through prediction. Critics such as Kuhn (1962) and Habermas (1974), however, have questioned this criterion by which theoretic assertions are to be accepted or rejected. Although they differ in important respects from one another, Kuhn and Habermas both reject the notion that correspondence is the straight-forward, mechanical and objective procedure claimed by advocates of the logico-deductive form. The entire scientific process is much more thoroughly social and the interpretation of the nature and degree of correspondence depends on complex patterns of understanding developed within social contexts. Knowledge claims – rather than resting upon mechanical procedures – are accepted or rejected in terms of criteria produced within relevant communities of participants. That is, knowledge claims are always interpreted and the interpretive process develops within the discourse of social settings. Even critics of this position, such as Popper or Lakatos and Musgrave (1970), agree that critical discourse is a central dimension of scientific activity, although they clearly regard rational discourse in less social terms than, for instance, Kuhn does. The production of theoretic knowledge can thus be viewed as a social process characterized by features found in other social contexts.

This alternative portrayal of scientific activity, emphasizing the importance of social discourse in the production of knowledge, implies that normative and moral concerns cannot be excluded from theorizing. Rather, they must be subjected to public discourse, though such a process does not assure certitude or even the attainment of a consensual judgement. A public discourse makes possible the enlargement and refinement of debate and the examination of alternative futures. Large-scale empirical issues need to be examined in terms of their relation to ultimate ends.

A related set of major criticisms of the logico-deductive conception of theory is directed at the presumption that it represents a neutral format in which competing theories can be assessed for their truth value. In order to employ the logico-deductive design, however, one does in fact make a large number of assumptions about the nature of the social world and the characteristics of human beings within it. For example, one must focus upon the kinds of problems that lend themselves to a certain form of empirical testing – usually measuring the extent of correspondence between theoretic values and observational values quantitatively expressed. But this is not a neutral requirement. It involves substantive assumptions that the essential nature of the social world has a particular quantitative and relational character. And in a similar sense, the objectivity requirement, separating the observer from that which is observed, embodies the substantive assumption that the social world is pre-existent to and independent of actors' conceptions and constructions of it. Further, such a world is presupposed to be substantively orderly and governed by regularities that can be expressed in general laws. Order and regularity are assumed to be properties of nature and are not dependent on any conscious or intentional action of human agents. Agents do not seriously affect the operation of this order. They may come to understand the nature of these forces, but the presuppositional basis of this conception rules out social creation or construction based on human reflectivity.

The positivist conception of theory thus makes sense only in the context of a rather elaborate set of assumptions about the nature of the social world and the ways social scientists can know this world. Once these assumptions are granted, the claims of objectivity and ethical and value-neutrality make sense and appear to inhere in the scientific method. The unproblematic acceptance of these kinds of assumptions permits its advocates to believe they are dealing with the facts of nature, because they have already accepted as given that the social world is empirically 'out there', a world that has properties independent of reflectively informed actions of human agents.

But, why should one accept these particular assumptions and the theoretical assertions based on them? Even empirical confirmation of the assertions could reasonably be doubted on the grounds that observations are theory-laden extensions of assertions and assumptions. And, even if we grant the independence of observations, the logico-deductive mode cannot discriminate between 'facts' that truly reflect some universal set of regularities and those which are consequences of the 'frozen relations of production'.

Sociological Theory as a Social Process

For our purposes, the most important conclusion to be drawn from an analysis of logico-deductive reasoning is that all conceptions of the nature of theory, as well as all substantive theories, contain a presuppositional base.[4] While there are other important components of theory that are generally unrecognized in this dominant conception, the most critical aspect is the infrastructure of domain assumptions from which theorists, as social agents, inevitably reason in formulating theoretic assertions and arguments about the nature of things in the social world. Our analysis of the social nature of logico-deductive theory parallels arguments developed in other contexts, by Michael Polanyi (1964), Alexandre Koyre (1968) and N. R. Hanson (1965), that it is not solely the order of the world nor its regularities that imprint this reality upon our sense apparatus. Rather, observations are possible only because we start with some conceptions about the fundamental nature of the world.

Theory, then, is a social process. The products of theorizing are anticipated in the fundamental assumptions and other infrastructural components, such as the logical forms of reasoning and assessment procedures, which guide the project as a whole.[5] What can be called a theory will always contain, at least at the infrastructural level, a particular configuration of elements mapping what is taken to be the nature of things. This configuration is the bedrock upon which the theoretical claims are made possible. Reasons for addressing social life in certain ways derive from these assumptions about 'what is' essentially the case. Theoretical infrastructures thus contain conceptions by which one makes sense of and orders the social world.

Perhaps most importantly, however, these fundamental assumptions about social reality and human nature contain moral orientations. To take an assumptive stance toward what is natural, normal and necessary also entails a moral posture about the correctness and desirability of that which is contained in the assumptions. As Robert Bellah (1983, p. 377) has suggested, 'What we say human beings fundamentally are has inevitable consequences for what they ought to be.' Theoretical assumptions thus embody a fundamental moral stance toward the world; theories are more than mere assertions about the magnitude of relations among things to be subjected to empirical testing. They are, basically, moral orientations to social life. For this reason, assumptions relative to the fundamental nature of collective social phenomena, social agents, and the relationships between agents and collectivities, not ordinarily explicated in a theory, are assertions deserving assessment in some public manner.

Moral Orientations in Sociological Theory

Having conceptualized theorizing as a social process in which moral orientations are embedded in the fundamental assumptions which theorists make about social reality, we will apply this conception by examining a few examples of classical and contemporary sociological theory. Classical theorists of the nineteenth and early twentieth centuries, though generally committed – as we have indicated – to some version of the scientific study of society, were nevertheless committed to addressing major historical issues of what is right and wrong with modern Western society. And each had a moral as well as a scientific orientation toward the proper direction of society they used to reflect upon the large-scale developments taking place in the Western world.

Of the classical sociological theorists, Marx (1967) most explicitly addressed the moral dimensions of modern capitalist society. His theoretical analysis of the empirical data on modern capitalism begins and ends with moral considerations. The content of Marx's analysis was predicated upon the observation that the great wealth of modern society accrued to the owners of production instead of the producers themselves and that this accumulation of wealth occurred both systematically and legally. But Marx conceived of the accumulation process as the moral problem of expropriation – a problem to be corrected through a transformation of society. His entire analysis, although couched in scientific terms and characterized by rigorous analysis, never deviates from the central moral theme. In truth, his moral problem derives from his conception of the fundamental nature of human agents and the best form of relationship among them.

Durkheim (1961, 1964) was less overtly political, but no less morally oriented, than Marx. The theme of Durkheim's work derives from the same general context – moral issues of modern society – that informs the work of Marx. He was, of course, quite explicit in his fundamental contention that society itself was a moral entity, an entity in which a collective identity existed because moral values and norms were generally shared by members of society. He identified the key moral value of modern Western society as 'ethical individualism', the collective ideal that provided the 'noncontractual element', in the exchange relations of capitalist organization. The conjunction of these features provided members of modern society with a double bond of integration. In as much as Durkheim asserted that more social integration was preferable to lesser forms of social solidarity, his overall moral orientation to modern society is evident.

Durkheim's fundamental reasoning also contains other moral predispositions. In making the basic assumption that society is prior to the individual, he structures the moral considerations of what the relationship between society and its members should be. For all the qualifications that one might adduce, the major thrust of his writing centers around the assumption that moral values and norms of existing society constitute the appropriate standards for directing human conduct.

Within the classical sociological tradition, Weber (1964) is perhaps the most difficult to locate in terms of fundamental moral orientations and commitments. This is somewhat paradoxical, for few thinkers of this period were as concerned with the moral nature of human existence in the twentieth century. Yet, Weber was ambivalent and ambiguous with respect to issues concerning the current human condition. On the one hand, it is Weber who provides the rationale for value-neutrality in the social science – the unbridgeable gulf between social ends and scientific means. But he also deals explicitly with ethical issues, both in his general treatment of religion, and in the more specific treatments of the ethics of responsibility and of ultimate ends.

Moreover, Weber was ambiguous in terms of his basic domain assumptions about social life. At a general theoretical level, he conceives of human actors as the creators of social action based upon subjectively interpreted meanings; social action is thus not coerced but oriented towards, and guided by, commitments to and interpretations of values. At other times, however, he sees the inevitable triumph of bureaucratic rationality controlling the fate of actors within the Western world. In Weber, we witness what appears to be an irresolvable conflict between science and ethics.

Yet, for all the tortured ambivalence permeating his work, a set of domain assumptions can be glimpsed. In the debate over the ethics of responsibility and the ethics of ultimate ends, and despite Weber's customary qualifications, it is reasonably clear that Weber opts for the ethics of responsibility as the realistic source of conduct within the modern state. In contrast to orienting conduct in terms of ultimate ethical ends, Weber repeatedly tells us that the appropriate ethical standard is the strategic norm of responsibility, where responsibility is identified in terms of political power in the existing state. That is, appropriate standards of conduct are those which coincide with the maintenance and improvement of the ongoing political order. While Weber is far too sophisticated to be regarded as a crass nationalist, his nationalism is prevalent in this context, as even many of his staunchest defenders have come to see. In resolving what an actor is realistically supposed to do, Weber reveals the underlying categories of his world view. This view patently contains Weber's moral justification of and commitment to modern capitalism and Western society.

Within contemporary sociological theory, Parsons (1951, 1967) stands out as a dominant intellectual figure. To a greater extent than the

European classical theorists, Parsons aspired to create scientific sociological theory. To be sure, Parsons modified his view on theory at various points in his career. But he seems to have generally accepted certain basic tenets of the positivist conception of theory: the necessity for empirical testing of theoretical assertions and the proscription of moral claims within theory. As with the classical figures it can be argued that Parsons's basic assumptions, as well as his general theoretical reasoning, although ambiguously presented, contain a pervasive moral orientation and commitment.

Parsons's substantive theorizing is most closely akin to that of Durkheim and Weber. And, while it does not contain the tortured ambivalence of Weber, it is perhaps even more ambiguous. Some critics have regarded Parsons's theoretical obscurantism as an intentional maneuver to avert the identification of the nature and source of the moral content of his substantive predispositions. As several critics have implied, the corpus of his work does appear to rest upon the assumption that the natural, and best, form of society exists in the categories underlying the American welfare state.

Parsons, like Durkheim, makes a fundamental assumption that society is prior to the individual. In working from this general assumption, society is elevated above the individual members. As preconditions for individual activity, society's maintenance becomes the fundamental prerequisite above all other social considerations, and integration of society becomes the guiding moral imperative. Individuals must be socialized to voluntarily comply (or else be constrained) with patterned actions that accomplish the requisite integration. In this general view, the individual is free when he/she acts in terms of the norms that promote cohesion and integration. The agent earns certain rights by satisfactorily complying with the normative order, but agents have no fundamental moral rights apart from the social order.

Parsons ultimately comes to use social system categories (those of the advanced welfare state) as the basis for evaluating social activity. The medically ill, for instance, are viewed from this detached position. Parsons theorizes about their 'condition' in relation to the overall management of society and not about them as people or the larger-scale processes by which they became deviant or ill. In effect, Parsons's concern for scientific theory disguises a morally laden infrastructure.

Another broad theoretical tradition in contemporary sociology, the micro-sociological perspective, also evinces moral orientations and commitments. The common theoretical focus in this broad perspective is the individual actor. Specific theories within the tradition are predicated upon differing assumptions of the nature of the human actor and these orient theorists to quite different moral positions. Actors may be conceived in subjective terms, for example, in symbolic interaction theory, or in objective terms exemplified by social exchange theory. In the former theoretical stance, actors are seen as creating and constructing the social world in alignment with their definitions of social phenomena. The latter position assumes that the individual acts in objective terms, that is, in terms of formal calculable forces located within the individual or impinging upon the individual externally. In either case, these kinds of assumptions are criss-crossed by other assumptions, such as those concerning the possibility of accounting for individual actions – whether considered subjectively or objectively – in terms of general laws of science. The kinds of assumptions made will dictate the extent to which the logico-deductive conception of theory is applicable. But almost independently of the notion of theory utilized, one finds the general eschewing of moral implications within the micro-sociological tradition.

The proscription of moral commitment comes out quite strongly in the version of micro-sociological theory that is often considered to be atheoretical or 'inductive'. An American example of this version is sometimes referred to as 'Midwestern empiricism' or the Wisconsin model of social inquiry. Its general nature has been succinctly captured: 'The work is essentially microsociological, focusing on individuals operating within structural constraints, rather than on structural constraints themselves. Throughout ... we are continually presented with the positivist version of sociology as an empirical science with clear application to the solution of social problems' (Hanneman, 1983, p. 639). Denial of political and moral elements does not hide the morality implied in the conception of individuals being acted upon in regularized ways by structural features. Failure to recognize and take this dimension into account only complicates understanding that the relation between scientific results and their application to social problems is inherently a moral and political project.

For all the diversity of theoretical reasoning within contemporary sociology, and for the diversity of moral orientations and commitments this would seem to imply, there appear to be certain common features with respect to the moral positions of Durkheim, Weber and Parsons. There is in particular the recurring theme of an ethics of duty or responsibility. That is, one has an ethical duty to act in terms of the moral categories of the society or state. In turn, one has certain rights bequeathed by the social order in relation to the performance of or compliance with these duties and responsibilities. Similarly, the implicit utilitarian ethics that undergird large sections of the micro-sociological perspective can be seen as a case of the ethics of duty. Actors' rights are contingent upon the proper performance of duties in the context of external constraints. Whether macro or micro, then, contemporary sociological theory tends to represent an administrative notion of cost–benefit analysis. The content of these theories portray a decision-making society in which human activity is assessed in mechanical terms on the basis of a responsible contribution to, or cost to, the general welfare of society, without any concern for the consequences to specific groups of individuals.

Human Rights Theory and the Classical Sociological Tradition

Although most sociologists continue to deny the existence of a moral component in their research and theory, we believe that, on both theoretical and empirical grounds, moral reasoning has, and continues to be, an integral part of sociological inquiry.[6] If this is so, and if sociologists are to understand human nature and social reality, as well as to contribute to the betterment of the human condition, some of the main features of the classical tradition must be reasserted. Like the classical theorists, we must analyze major empirical issues in the modern world within a broad theoretical framework – one that makes explicit our moral presuppositions as social scientists and as human beings.

This calls for recasting the theoretical issues addressed by Marx, Durkheim, Weber and Parsons because new empirical realities have arisen which these scholars could not have meaningfully understood. The nation-state and its elaborate administrative apparatus, which most classical sociologists typically accepted as morally sound, has itself become a moral dilemma. The Nazis' systematic destruction of European Jews (and their rampant experimentation with human subjects in the name of science) as well as the Soviet Gulags are obvious cases in point. And modern science, which has been integrated into the bureaucratic structures of nation-states, has given rise to such empirical and moral issues as the potential destruction of humankind through nuclear holocaust. In addition, problems facing the dispossessed in the Third World are associated with the power alignments of nation-states in the larger world system.

The basic moral thrust of the classical tradition of Durkheim and Weber, as well as Parsons, also requires reformulation. We must look beyond the traditional ethical concern with duties, particularly with respect to the nation-state. Instead, we emphasize a morality of human rights which we argue to be more fundamental than duties. We build upon, but basically revise, the theorizing about human rights by such scholars as Dworkin (1977).[7] In seeking to answer the question posed by Bellah and his colleagues, 'what is the morality that should guide social science?' (1983, p. 17), we maintain that sociologists should participate with others in the construction of a new moral stance for theorizing based on human rights extended to all humankind. Here, we can only present a highly adumbrated account of what the infrastructure for that theorizing might be like.

Human agents and social structures are fundamental components of social reality which, we argue, cannot be reduced to one another, although they do not exist without one another (Vaughan and Sjoberg, 1984). Agents and structures are bound together in terms of dialectical tension that is historically variable, agents sometimes coming to the fore but more often resisting the domination of institutions and organizations. This appears to be a more defensible portrayal of social reality than those assumptions giving primacy to individual characteristics (such as individual self-interest in social exchange theory), or those theories assuming the individual is a product of social arrangements over which one has no control (such as normative functionalism).

We take the capacity for social reflectivity to be the most essential characteristic of humankind. This capacity, socially shaped and developed within particular institutions and structures, instills the potential to transcend particular settings. It is this capacity, to simultaneously shape and be shaped by social reality, that is the distinguishing feature of humanness – the capacity, problematic though it may be, to be consciously aware of the process of reflectivity. This is not to argue that human agents escape the imperatives of institutions and organizations, but the range of social phenomena is not limited by what currently exists or what historical laws produce. Furthermore, social arrangements can promote or deny reflectivity. Thus, reflectivity and the social conditions necessary for its expression must become ethical concerns. Organizational and institutional forms that facilitate the greatest expression of reflectivity are socially and morally superior forms of organization. Organizational forms that constrain and limit reflectivity are socially and morally inferior. We extend our contentions, moreover, that agents can never be totally reduced to organizational imperatives nor organizations reduced to agents' activities and that a basic tension exists between agents and organizations, to hold for human activity across all socio-cultural settings.

On the basis of this reasoning we can now explicate the basic moral principles implicated by this theoretical infrastructure. As the fundamental feature of human status, all human beings have a basic and socially inalienable right to reflective consciousness, independently of any other consideration. Thus, no person, group or organization has a right to deprive any human being of the human status of social reflectivity. That is, the capacity to reason in terms of alternatives should not be contingent upon the performance of duties or obligations. One does not earn or merit this right through performance of duties, nor is it part of an external bargaining system.

A second basic moral principle following from our theoretical infrastructure is the right to the social conditions of reflectivity. Since reflective consciousness is a potential only realizable in social contexts, every person and group rightfully should have access to the necessary social structures for developing and sustaining reflective consciousness whereby one achieves human status. The right to human status – including a social reflectivity and the facilitative social arrangements necessary to sustain it – is fundamental. The denial of human status, such as genocide, slavery and apartheid, reduces persons to 'objects'. It follows from this position that no person, group, or organization, including the nation-state, should deny any other person or group the conditions of human status and human dignity.

While the right to human status may appear to be somewhat similar to Kant's (1956) notion of each individual as an inherently valuable end, our formulation differs from Kant's (and that of other philosophers who conceive of persons in highly individualistic terms). We must look beyond the pre-social categories of Kant, if we are to come to terms with what it means to be human within the context of social structures. It then follows that we must hold not only human agents, but organizations as well, morally accountable. If such practices as genocide and triage are to be eliminated, we must construct a moral orientation where the right to human status cannot be manipulated by any organization, including the nation-state.

Violations of human status occur under many circumstances. In modern societies, the most serious and systematic threats to human status occur most often in large-scale bureaucratic structures. Bureaucracies are moral phenomena because they are organized on principles that run counter to social reflectivity and enhancement of human status. Bureaucracies systematically operate to reduce social reflectivity by severely limiting the options that one has for response within the bureaucratic setting. One's place in a bureaucratic structure is primarily geared to the accomplishment of the non-reflectively produced goals and interests of others. Indeed, the bureaucracy can and does resort to power and coercion to accomplish the ends of some at the expense of others.

Conclusions

We have argued, in effect, that the positivist perspective, which has sought to replace the classical sociological tradition, is unable to examine the major social and moral issues in the modern world. Moreover, positivists in practice sustain moral orientations such as those associated with utilitarianism, nation-state morality, and relativism, but they persistently ignore this aspect of their theoretical project.

We believe, while it is necessary to restore aspects of classical theorizing, a new theoretical project informed by a human rights rather than a duties orientation should be introduced. The strategy we have suggested would clearly transform the essential nature of empirical and theoretical activity in sociology. It would emphasize the promotion of conditions that enable human beings to maximize social reflectivity. If sociologists are to address the great issues of our age, they must not passively accept and reinforce 'what is' – a moral stance in and of itself – but they must actively engage in the construction of new and more human social arrangements. This would permit sociologists to re-engage themselves in a noble calling that is in keeping with their heritage.

Notes

1 Although many contemporary sociologists acknowledge that the ethics of social research is a legitimate concern, they persist in the failure to examine the moral orientations and commitments of sociologists – theorists as well as researchers. Alexander, 1982, for example, uses the term 'moral' on various occasions, but he does not analyze the moral dimensions of the theories he investigates. In addition to the brief survey herein, see some of our other writings – e.g. Sjoberg, Vaughan and Sjoberg, 1984, and Vaughan and Sjoberg, 1984 – for a tentative examination of some of the moral dimensions of sociological inquiry.

2 In order to be as precise as possible about the acceptance of terms and statements in the logico-deductive version of scientific theory, the theoretic/observation and analytic/synthetic distinctions were introduced by members of the Vienna Circle, especially Carnap. For a discussion of these dichotomies, see Suppe, 1977, especially pp. 45–53 and 66–86.

3 The dominance of logical positivism (or empiricism) in contemporary American sociology has its analog in philosophy where the positivists or analytical philosophers came to dominate the major departments of philosophy. See, for example, Rorty, 1982. In practice, however, the logico-deductive format is less frequently used than other logical forms such as the logic of discovery, analogy, the dialectic (in its various forms), and classification and typification.

4 We define social theory as a process that involves three dimensions – domain assumptions, the logical forms of reasoning and inquiry, and assessment procedures. Because domain assumptions or presuppositions (terms we employ synonymously) seem more basic in carrying the moral premises of social theory than logical forms and assessment procedures, we have focused our attention in this essay on this facet of social theorizing.

5 In differentiating between process and product, we must realize that various domain assumptions in sociological theorizing are often intentionally concealed from public examination. Present day theorists usually gloss over these fundamental issues. One often gains a fuller understanding of these assumptions by reading book reviews rather than the *American Sociological Review*. It is often necessary to place theorists in their historical setting, so as to understand their biographies, if we are to understand how and why they have argued as they have.

6 Sorokin, 1947, is an exception to the idea that contemporary theorists avoid articulating a moral perspective.

7   There is a vast body of legal and political theory dealing with human rights that has yet to find its way into sociology. Of current writers, Dworkin's work seems to be the most useful point of departure, although it stands in need of major revision. For an overview of these issues, see Cohen, 1984.

10

Hermeneutics and Axiology: the Ethical Contents of Interpretation

Alan Sica

It is bad enough to learn from Richard Rorty that what is worth knowing in Foucault's *Order of Things* about 'rationality, objectivity, method, and truth' was already given out more lucidly and, as a bonus, with 'a kind of hope', in *Human Nature and Conduct* sixty years ago (Rorty, 1982, pp. 204, 206). But even worse, for social theorists, is Robert Bellah's claim that Randall Collins's 'revolutionary' effort to systematize an important type of current thinking, in *Conflict Sociology*, predicates itself on 'fundamental principles ... identical with those in Book I of *Leviathan*, published by Hobbes in 1651'; that the newer book amounts to 'significant omissions, reworkings, and waterings down' (Bellah, 1983, pp. 375–6). Bellah suggests we call what we do 'moral sciences', and that we elevate our capabilities to do it by reading the *Republic* ('a profound analysis of social life that simultaneously illuminates as perhaps no other work does the ethical ends of human action' [p.362]), Aristotle's joint production, the *Ethics* and *Politics*, Machiavelli's *Prince* and *Discourses*, *Leviathan*, and Tocqueville's *Democracy in America*, all in anticipation of Durkheim or Weber regarding 'the good life'. About the *Discourses* Bellah says that it

> is not an ethical injunction without cognitive analysis; it is the moral passion that opens the space for cognitive analysis – the two are inseparable. Therefore, Machiavelli's work is at the same time a profound analysis of the nature of certain kinds of societies (in fact, more can be learned about the current problems of the American republic from his *Discourses* than from any contemporary work of American political science), a reflection (largely implicit) about the ends of man, and an effort at persuasion that the ends he desires are admirable and attainable (in the highest and truest sense, it is a work of

rhetoric ... in its combination of the analytic, the ethical, and the rhetorical, Machiavelli resembles Plato and Aristotle). (Bellah, 1983, pp. 363–4)

Bellah's endorsement of classical thought extends still further: 'Hobbes's powerful and in some respects unsurpassed social psychology (foreshadowed by Augustine and elaborated by Freud) had a profound moral implication and purpose' (1983, p. 364); Tocqueville's 'book is unrivaled as an analysis of a total society, culture, and modal personality and of how they fit together. But it is always ethical and political in its intent and a superb example of rhetoric' (p. 365).

It comes as no surprise, then, when Bellah finds in Durkheim – whom he prefers as a morally engaged sociologist to Weber ('riven with inner tensions' [1983, p. 371]) – a student and propagandist on behalf of 'practical reason' very much in the Greek tradition, even though he did what he could to protect the 'facade of science' (p. 367) against the potent incursions of axiology. Like so many, Durkheim wanted to tame our major antinomy, to profit a private moral vision of modern life by contact with the public, pristine scientific method. And, like nearly everyone, one side of his ledger accordingly gained as the other lost. But perhaps this need not be the case as the struggle for supremacy between ethics and science begins, apparently, to wind down. Meanwhile, though, note the vocabulary Bellah bravely smuggles into his commentary on social theory: 'ethical ends of man'; 'moral passion that opens the space for cognitive analysis'; 'a superb example of rhetoric'; 'a profound moral implication and purpose'. Can *any* contemporary social theory, even one like Habermas's which overtly speaks to 'moral development' and reconstruction, be described using such terms? The question answers itself. For those who share Bellah's preferences, it stands as an indictment of our moral and intellectual irresponsibility. But for other denizens of the post-Kuhnian environment, where dangerous subjectivity undercuts shopworn claims for scientific objectivity, Bellah's type of rhetoric is as irrelevant to social science as it is dangerous to its image.

It seems that philosophers currently have more to say that is useful concerning these problems – of important ideas buried in forgotten books, and of the language necessary to embrace them – than one can find in journals published for sociologists. One of the most incisive is Rorty. As already noted, he shares Bellah's reservations about contemporary social thought. For example, he makes a plausible case that Foucault's particular type of 'narrative and anecdotal style' (1982, p. 203), while long on a 'tone' that is 'a self-dramatizing Continental one' (p. 205), is short on helping us out of our current dilemmas. Dewey, in sharp contrast, began with the premise that what is intellectually exciting is only so to the extent that it is of some analytic or practical use – better yet, both. People will argue that Rorty's end point, another celebration of liberal democratic values, vitiates his preceding argument. But for the social scientist/moral philosopher interested in how axiology suddenly found itself in a previously unimaginable position – fenced outside the academy, looking in at intellectual labors putatively about humans but resolved to forego ultimate values as 'unscientific' – Rorty's arguments against current pessimisms promise something. Similarly with Bellah (and other contributors to *Social Science as Moral Inquiry*), a case is made that only after rapprochement with classical authors is accomplished, for whom social analysis was *ipso facto* axiological, can contemporary writers come to the aid of a culture with plenty of technology and little humanity, and a technocratic mode of domination for which ethical choices 'do not compute'. Such sentiments, pleading for a return to sources more generously attentive to life-as-lived than those social 'science' has produced of late, is not romanticization of classical texts and their authors. It is a reminder, one which resurfaces in crises times, that the determining items of axiological concern do not vary much from social structure to social structure, because our physical and emotional make-up stretches only so far; not far enough, one could argue, to mend the tears inflicted by scientistic reductions of existence, ethics and being, and likewise by their wayward disciple, mechanical modernity.

Since social inquiry is itself a product of the pervasive formal rationalization, it has not escaped the 'bad infinite' (Gadamer, 1983, p. 40), the axiological void that chokes the rest of contemporary intellectualism. If in 1970 Gouldner was social theory's solo Cassandra, today we hear a complete chorus, each member harmonizing around several dominant motifs. In 'Raiders of the lost paradigm' (a title sure to mystify the future), Peter Lassman has assessed much of the current 'crisis' literature within social theory, and has highlighted examples of this persistent theme. Frank Parkin points out the ' "virtual disintegration" of the "inner core" of general sociological theory' (Lassman, 1982, p. 291), and Steven Lukes wonders if such theory, because of its inherent conceptual confusion, can ever hope to establish 'autonomy' from culture at large. In an important paper from another volume, Norbert Wiley (1979) speaks of an 'interregnum' that has stalled theoretical advance, with Marxism, quantified applied work, and exhausted functionalism, among doctrines, limping through journals as the weary standards they have become (Lassman, 1982, p. 295). But most germane to the present volume is Lassman's own opinion.

The image created by all of these analyses and discussions is one of a linguistic maze within which 'critiques' of sociology are written in the same sociological language which is being criticized ... When we stand outside of the maze we realize that sociological thought degenerates into technical triviality or empty generality when it lacks a unifying moral and political vision. (1982, p. 298)

Out of the 'rather *chaotic pluralism*' that a National Science Foundation executive saw in sociology today, one can scarcely hope for a unified axiological vision (cited in Wiley, 1979, p. 74; original emphasis). But since many participants and observers concerned with sociology's apparent demise – at the center of which, I would argue, is its theoretical emptiness – agree that some moral and/or political forthrightness might do the discipline good, I propose forgetting for the moment the half-dozen schools of the 1960s and 1970s, and turning to hermeneutics in an effort to regain theoretical acuity and axiological direction. Whatever inconsistencies surround the word itself, hermeneutics has found a pivotal place in social thought over the last decade in the works of Habermas, Giddens, Rorty and others, and of late has allowed its grand old man, Gadamer, to enter the sphere of social theory *per se* by way of ontology and aesthetics.

Rationality and Reason

As a beginning, let us accept Rorty's lead and think again about today's arid formulations of rationality and the 'reasonable' alongside the less timid or scientistic proposals by forefathers of our thought, William James, Nietzsche and Dewey. In the perennial best-seller, *Pragmatism* (1907), James gave to the laity an anti-epistemology they could understand and appreciate. He followed his colleagues F. C. S. Schiller and Dewey in spreading the 'new name for some old ways of thinking' by defining 'truth' thus: 'It means, they say, nothing but this, *that ideas (which themselves are but parts of our experience) become true just in so far as they help us to get into satisfactory relation with other parts of our experience*, to summarize them and get about among them by conceptual short-cuts instead of following the interminable succession of particular phenomena' (James, 1907, p. 58, original emphasis). The word 'rationality' does not figure heavily in James's text, but in the sense I am proposing, as a necessary factor in hermeneutic enterprise, it suffuses all his anti-epistemology. In fact, when he does ask 'what *kind* of a reason can there ultimately be', he separates '*living reason*' from the 'secondarily rational shape', arguing that the former 'is *demanded* – ... to give relief to no matter how small a fraction of the world's mass'. Such pure demands pushing for instant satisfaction dominate 'the Absolute's own world', that is, utopia, but within the worldly framework of 'pluralistic moralism', filled as it is with perpetual compromises, the philosophically lesser form of rationality prevails (James, 1907, pp. 288–93; original emphasis). But the steering mechanism, imprecise to be sure, common to this system of the 'secondarily rational shape' is a congeries of 'true ideas' which 'lead us into useful verbal and conceptual quarters as well as directly up to useful sensible termini. They lead to consistency, stability and flowing human intercourse. They lead away from excentricity [sic] and isolation, from foiled and barren thinking' (James, 1907, p. 215). With rhetoric this strong, expressing its own 'healthy-minded buoyancy' (p. 291), it is small wonder that in Rorty's (1979) major work James's unique philosophical language (such as the 'cash-value' of ideas) quietly established itself as the foil against which more recent, feeble jargons were measured.

Note how unperturbed James was with what we now would call the 'issue' of values. For him ideas are true if they abet the locating of this 'satisfactory relation with other parts of our experience' that he uses as an epistemological foundation. He does not worry much about what *precisely* 'satisfactory relations' might mean to this or that constituency, to 'our' experiences. He seems to assume that discovering, defining and experiencing such arrangements, those that at once embody and reveal 'reason', is not the great block to philosophical or existential meaning that academic philosophy and social science have made it over the past forty years or so. In short, he is refusing to believe than an axiological grounding for human life is so difficult to come by that professional thinkers and analysts must hide from it to protect their aspirations for 'scientific' reliability, objectivity, truth, or whatever term suits their sacred ideal.

In this he shares a fundamental belief with Dewey, whose lyrical portrait of reason's place in science, and vice-versa, stands among the most memorable passages in his most widely read book.

Rationality, once more, is not a force to evoke against impulse and habit. It is the attainment of a working harmony among diverse desires. 'Reason' as a noun signifies the happy cooperation of a multitude of dispositions, such as sympathy, curiosity, exploration, experimentation, frankness, pursuit – to follow things through – circumspection, to look about at the context, etc., etc. The elaborate systems of science are born not of reason but of impulses at first slight and flickering; impulses to handle, move about, to hunt, to uncover, to mix things separated and to divide things combined, to talk and to listen. Method is their effectual organization into continuous dispositions of inquiry, development and testing. It occurs after these acts and because of their consequences. Reasons, the rational attitude, is the resulting disposition, not a ready-made antecedent which can be invoked at will and set into movement. The man who would intelligently cultivate intelligence will widen, not narrow, his life of strong impulses while aiming at their happy coincidence in operation. (Dewey, 1930, p. 196)

Here is striking kinship with Gadamer's hermeneutic understanding, especially the emphasis Dewey gives to the desire 'to talk and to listen' and the correlative willingness to include rather than flee from various impulses and world views; what Gadamer, following Heidegger, identifies as an 'openness to Being' that accompanies effective interpretation (Gadamer, 1975, pp. 235ff.). Perhaps Dewey's apprenticeship in Hegelianism, though far behind him by 1922, had engendered a refusal to close the 'floodgates' of knowledge (as Max Scheler called them), so that his project – as was Gadamer's – became one of progressive exploration and opening, while other philosophers fascinated themselves by contracting their conceptual worlds, taking in less and less, and then saying more and more about it.

Rorty is memorably pungent regarding the supersedure of pragmatism by less invigorating philosophies of inquiry, and his objections match Gadamer's, though originating in very different sources.

What Foucault doesn't give us is what Dewey wanted to give us – a kind of hope which doesn't *need* reinforcement from 'the idea of a transcendental or enduring subject' ... Foucault sees no middle ground, in thinking about the social sciences, between the 'classic' Galilean conception of 'behavioral sciences' and the French notion of '*sciences de l'homme*'. It was just such a middle ground that Dewey proposed, and which inspired the social sciences in America before the failure of nerve which turned them 'behavioral'. More generally, the recent reaction in favor of hermeneutical social sciences ... has taken for granted that if we don't want something like Parsons, we have to take something like Foucault; i.e., that overcoming the deficiencies of Weberian *Zweckrationalitaet* requires going all the way, repudiating the 'will to truth'. What Dewey suggested was that we keep the will to truth and the optimism that goes with it, but free them from the behaviorist notion that Behaviorese is Nature's Own Language *and* from the notion of man as 'transcendental or enduring subject'. For, in Dewey's hands, the will to truth is not the urge to dominate but the urge to create, to 'attain working harmony among diverse desires'. (Rorty, 1982, pp. 206–7)

This passage not only consolidates points made earlier, but questions Dewey's obsolescence in terms completely at one with today's hermeneutic critique of social science. (Other matters are also raised, to which I will return.)

Finally Rorty reminds us of how Nietzsche anticipated Foucault and others who took Sophism seriously, in connecting high-flown truth-seeking with the simple facts of domination.

> The criterion of truth resides in the enhancement of the feeling of power ... Toward an understanding of logic: *the will to equality is the will to power* – the belief that something is thus and thus (the essence of *judgement*) is the consequence of a will that as much as possible *shall* be equal ... The conceptual ban on contradiction proceeds from the belief that we are *able* to form concepts, that the concept not only designates the essence of a thing but *comprehends* it – In fact, logic (like geometry and arithmetic) applies only to fictitious entities that we have created. Logic is the attempt to comprehend the actual world by means of a scheme of being posited by ourselves; more correctly, to make it formulateable and calculable for us. (Nietzsche, 1967, pp. 290, 277, 280)

There is also a genuine link between Nietzsche's anti-methodological ideas and pragmatism: the 'mistake of philosophy is that, instead of seeing logic and the categories of reasons and means for fixing up the world or utilitarian ends ... one thinks that they give one a criterion of truth about *reality*' (Nietzsche, quoted by Rorty, 1982, p. 205). In the same work I quoted above, Nietzsche assumes the self-dramatizing continental posture Rorty noted in Foucault, and takes his epistemological de-construction to the brink, far beyond the healthy skepticism of either James or Dewey.

> Means of enduring it [the idea of eternal recurrence]: the revaluation of all values. No longer joy in certainty but in uncertainty; no longer 'cause and effect' but the continually creative; no longer will to preservation but to power; no longer the humble expression, 'everything is *merely* subjective', but 'it is also *our* work! – Let us be proud of it!'. (Nietzsche, 1967, p. 545)

This is the epistemological tone Lukács reviled in *The Destruction of Reason* (1980, pp. 309–99) because of its refusal to recognize societal constraints on consciousness or, more importantly for him and many others, on political awareness and action. Yet Rorty is right in reminding us of Dewey, James and Nietzsche in this context, when even the largest lights in our intellectual parlor now burn so low and tentatively. 'Edifying' though the 'peripheral philosophers' may be – Rorty includes in this grouping Derrida, the most cynical of today's thinkers regarding 'systematic' thought (Rorty, 1979, pp. 367–8) – fundamental decisions or realizations about values, ethics, the whole axiological domain, do not spring from mere edification and suspicion. They do indeed come from an 'urge to create', an urge to find that elusive harmony among diverse desires and to help us get into more satisfying relation with those aspects of experience that currently chafe.

Gouldner, Plato and Reason

Leaving Rorty's older favorites for the moment, we have hardly exhausted this century's contributions to the joint problem of rationality and interpretation. In his most astonishing and informative book, *Enter Plato*, Gouldner opens a crucial chapter entitled 'The fatigue of reason and the metaphysics of authoritarianism' (1965, p. 326) by quoting the man who gave him the title, Whitehead. Even if his metaphysical system is not entirely plausible, Whitehead went further in sensibly reconciling the claims of reason and its others – 'living reason' versus the 'secondarily rational shape' – than anyone in the modern period. He accomplished this through simplicity, quite in the style of James and Dewey, and not by proposing unwieldy or unrealistic axiomatic reductions. 'The function of Reason is to promote the art of life' is Whitehead's opening to his small book on the subject (Whitehead, 1958, p. 40). It is odd that the coauthor of *Principia Mathematica* should speak of the 'art of life', not of experimental truth, induction, hypothesis-testing, formal modelling, or the other grails of contemporary scientism. He actually opposes most of what passes as scientific method, especially among researchers in the *Geisteswissenschaften*.

> We have got to remember the two aspects of Reason, the Reason of Plato and the Reason of Ulysses, Reason as seeking a complete understanding and Reason as seeking an immediate method of action … The man with a method good for purposes of his dominant interests, is a pathological case in respect to his wider judgement on the coordination of this method with a more complete experience … the trained body of physiologists under the influence of the ideas germane to their successful methodology entirely ignore the whole mass of adverse evidence. We have here a colossal example of anti-empirical dogmatism arising from a successful methodology. Evidence which lies outside the method simply does not count. (Whitehead, 1958, pp. 11, 15)

Whitehead thus counterposes method and rationality. Like other more or less kindred thinkers, he finds stiff methodology incompatible with reason since the latter takes in life as such, not this or that manageable parcel. He elaborates this gentle polemic against narrowness in a semi-aphoristic style that recalls Adorno's more bitter denunciations of positivist blindness.

The primitive deep-seated satisfaction derived from Reason ... is provided by the emphatic clarification of some method regulating current practice. The method works and Reason is satisfied. There is no interest beyond the scope of the method. Indeed this last statement is too restrained. There is active interest restraining curiosity within the scope of the method. Any defeat of that interest arouses an emotional resentment. Empiricism vanishes ... The main evidence that a methodology is worn out comes when progress within it no longer deals with main issues. There is a final epoch of endless wrangling over minor question. (Whitehead, 1958, pp. 17–18)

These last remarks describe sociology's state with chilling accuracy. For nearly twenty years quantified methods in sociology – from factor analysis through path analysis to multiple regression, log-linear transformation, smallest-space analysis, and the permutations upon these which specialists debate and practitioners fear – have squelched curiosity among social researchers. They knew in advance that if their 'findings' could not be stated in terms of the technique fashionable in that year, room would not be found for them in journals. When one looks at the subjects treated 'empirically' by professional sociologists in these journals, or even the slightly broader issues broached by theorists, and then reflects upon the full dimensions of social life, Whitehead's observations take on the sound of a eulogy for the discipline. He capsulizes it beautifully: 'The birth of a methodology is in its essence the discovery of a dodge to live' (Whitehead, 1958, p. 18).

Whitehead, as author of epigraphs, has decorated numerous works of social theory, but Gouldner's choice for *Enter Plato* is more penetrating and anti-scientistic than those chosen by other writers.

'Fatigue' is the antithesis of Reason. The operations of Fatigue constitute the defeat of Reason in its primitive character of reaching after the upward trend. Fatigue means the operation of excluding the impulse toward novelty. It excludes the opportunities of the immediate stage at which life finds itself ... The inertia weighing upon Reason is generation of a mere recurrent round of change, unrelieved by novelty. The urge of Reason, clogged with such inertia, is fatigue ... There has been a relapse into mere repetitive life, concerned with mere living and divested of any factor involving effort towards living well, and still less of any effort towards living better. (Whitehead, 1958, pp. 23–4)

Gouldner complements the passage he quoted (a part of this excerpt) by choosing a later line from the book: 'The power of going for the penetrating idea, even if it has not yet been worked into any methodology, is what constitutes the progressive force of Reason. The great Greeks had this knack to an uncanny degree' (1965, p. 45). Gouldner omits the next several lines: 'The men of the thirteenth century had it. The men of the tenth century lacked it. In between them lay three centuries of speculative philosophy.' Gouldner's admiration for the Greek approach to thought and social organization is shared by Gadamer, who has joined his life-long study of Plato with attention to Aristotle, Hegel and Heidegger in order to rediscover 'the right way to live' (as his translator put it; Gadamer, 1983, pp. xi, xiv); to find that balance between *logos* and *ergon* at the center of Socrates's life (Gadamer, 1980, pp. 1–20), and which men of the tenth and twentieth centuries somehow misplaced. In *Enter Plato* Gouldner was after much the same thing, and it is important to recall that this book directly preceded his *Coming Crisis of Western Sociology* in which he explained why, as it were, Parsons was no Plato.

But even with Gouldner, as philosophically and politically circumspect a social theorist as the USA has produced since the Second World War, a marked weakening from the certainty of James, Dewey, Nietzsche and Whitehead – and their inspirers, Hegel and the Greeks – begins to reshape the notions of rationality, the reasonable and how one interprets them. There is a decided backing-off, perhaps even an extension of that 'failure of nerve' Rorty pointed out regarding the behaviorists earlier in this century, when the fundamental question of rational knowing and acting can no longer be held at bay. Just after quoting the Whitehead epigraph, Gouldner hesitates.

> It is, however, no easier to say what Plato's 'reason' is than to characterize that concept as it is used today in contemporary philosophical discourse; then as now reason is not a single but a multidimensional thing. It is clear, however, that the way Plato alludes to it, that reason is an elemental and approbative state of mind. It is a complex way of thinking, the full resources of which cannot be seen at a glance but have to be explored patiently and revealed piecemeal as each different context allows. (Gouldner, 1965, p. 326)

This is no longer the unrestrained *Lebensphilosophie* that Schleiermacher bequeathed to Dilthey, or that, in American dress, Dewey and James (even Mead) joyously made our official belief-system. Instead one meets sophisticated equivocation.

Gouldner says that Plato's 'reason' is a 'state of mind', a 'complex way of thinking'. But what we learn even from differing schools of Plato studies, for example, Gadamer's or Werner Jaeger's, is that '*phronesis*' (practical wisdom) and '*sophia*' (theoretical wisdom) derive from a special combination of *nous* (reason) and experience that transcends the merely or statically cognitive (Gadamer, 1975, p. 20). As Jaeger pointed out, Greek reason grew through an uneasy modification of religious myth, but that 'mythical thought without formative logic is blind, and logical theorizing without living mythical thought is empty' (Jaeger, 1945, p. 152). Moreover, in the golden age of Greek culture, rebellions against 'cold rationalism' flourished, as artists and thinkers began to see the dangers of substituting brute cognition – which is what pure rationality becomes – for evaluation of a more encompassing type (1945, p. 376).

But it is elsewhere in this work that Gouldner expresses a conceptualization of rationality that fits comfortably within sociology's self-understanding today, and is therefore even further distanced from the hermeneutic and axiological version familiar to Gadamer's readers. In an important section of *The Hellenic World* on Greek contests, Gouldner writes with Weberian tone in as much as the 'total-commitment rationality' of Athenian life is practically synonymous with the *zweckrationalisches Handelns* that his predecessor attributed to modernity:

> rationalism is an orientation in which the relation between means and ends is subject to deliberate calculation; in which ends or goals are constituted as perceptually organized foci set off from the contextual ground in which they are embedded; and in which other aspects of the surround [*sic*] are also taken from their context and evaluated primarily in terms of their anticipated capacity to realize the goal. In short, the more rational the orientation, the more might be said that the world is seen from the center comprised by the viewing person, and that elements in it are of significance primarily in terms of *his* progress. Rationalism thus premises an individual-centered world, in which the self can move easily in and out of the field of objects, choosing some to which it will make more enduring goal attachments ... The Greek capacity to disengage the self from sentimental attachments to persons meant that persons could then be used instrumentally ... or could be treated as interchangeable parts. (Gouldner, 1965, pp. 70–1)

Leaving aside the question of whether Gouldner's understanding of Greek social life is historically adequate, his portrait meshes handily with Weber's least appealing category of action, and surely is most at odds with Gadamer's (and Schleiermacher's) recovery of the Platonic and Aristotelian heritage. It would hardly be to a culture infatuated with 'total-commitment rationality' that one would go, at least by Gadamer's values, in order to discover how *logos* and *ergon* interact toward the creation of a rational polity. We see, then, that even a scholar of Gouldner's capacity could be hoodwinked into theoretical anachronism, heeding the father of modern action theory too well perhaps, and imagining how *hubris* was allowed, even encouraged, to triumph over *phronesis*, not to mention *sophia*, in Attic axiology.

Lessons of the Past

Had Gadamer's sixty years of Greek study been able merely to show Athens as a place of calculated aggrandizement, Habermas would not have said in his *laudatio* for him that in his study of the classics he had achieved a 'magnificent actualization of the humanist tradition' by unmasking the 'putative opposition between methodologically rigorous science and practical reason' and 'the false opposition between the metaphysical and the modern apprehension of the world' (Habermas, 1983b, pp. 196, 193). And, as Habermas well knows, it is this refusal to participate in 'degrading the tradition of the Greeks' (p. 197), especially regarding ultimate values like rationality and virtue, that has primed the hermeneutic critique of contemporary consciousness since before Schleiermacher.

What I have in mind, of course, is the monumental labor of Schleiermacher (begun with Schlegel) in translating Plato into German for the first time around 1800, and the introductions he wrote for the *Dialogues* (Schleiermacher, 1973). His hermeneutic theorizing grew out of 'his long practical experience', as Niebuhr put it (1964, p. 24), and was not something concocted *ad hoc*. Since I have given the rudiments of Schleiermacher's hermeneutic strategy elsewhere (Sica, 1981, pp. 42–8), I will use this opportunity instead to consider his *Hermeneutics* (Schleiermacher, 1977; written between 1805 and 1833) from an angle more germane to the present topic.

In Niebuhr's uniquely useful book, he correctly attaches Schleiermacher's technical expertise as a virtuoso interpreter of texts to a much larger, more important aspect of his life, his work as theologian and moralist. In one section of his book, aptly entitled 'The art of interpretation' (recalling Dewey and Rorty on the nature of hermeneutic labor), Niebuhr makes the same point I have in mind.

A distinguishing feature of Schleiermacher's ethics is its capacity to serve both as a philosophy of history, hence as a comprehensive interpretation of human thoughts and acts, and as a positive basis for particular historical sciences. Nowhere are the realism and the creativity of the ethics better shown than in the lectures on hermeneutics, or the art of interpretation. In fact, Schleiermacher lectured on ethics and hermeneutics concurrently, thereby demonstrating his own maxim that the general and the particular disciplines can grow in depth as well as scope only when they grow apace. (Niebuhr, 1964, p. 77)

Of the nineteen volumes that make up Dilthey's *Gesammelte Schriften*, four take up Schleiermacher's life and work, of which only a snippet is in English (Dilthey, 1976, pp. 37–77). If the architect of modern hermeneutics was indispensable to Dilthey, who in turn designed *verstehende* social science, certainly this centrality to thought has not slipped into our own day through the filters that Gadamer and Habermas each made. This needs rectification. Surely we cannot embrace Schleiermacher's religiosity or his polite naïveté about certain aspects of social life still feasible in Goethe's time. But in his ability and willingness to make interpretation itself a moral act – 'Interpretation, Schleiermacher was convinced ... is rooted in the constitution of man as an ethical agent' (Niebuhr, 1964, p. 80) – we can re-enter the axiological sphere in a way that Rorty accepts, but that Habermas fears. Schleiermacher believed that 'the original situation of the rational self is then a dialogical one' (Niebuhr, 1964, p. 81), which is a basic tenet of Gadamer's hermeneutics, and is also taken up by Habermas in his theory of communicative action. But whereas Schleiermacher, not unlike Rorty in this respect, or even Dewey, cheerfully understood that life is simply an hermeneutical exercise, a perpetual effort to minimize inevitable misunderstandings of others' particularity, in their speech, text and actions, and that it is a moral duty to work up one's hermeneutic skills to accomplish this, Habermas sticks to science, calling over and over for universal standards of rationality built on some more or less 'objective ground'.

Schleiermacher was utterly aware that *Streitigkeit* – conflict – the workings of dialectic in all its ferocity, had to be accepted as a given of existence, but Habermas and others betray 'a desire for constraint – a desire to find "foundations" to which one might cling, frameworks beyond which one must not stray, objects which impose themselves, representation which cannot be gainsaid' (Rorty, 1979, p. 315). There is in all this an anxiety associated with disagreement, with lack of consensus or even the grounds for establishing consensus, that is truly a 'gentleman's concept of hermeneutics' – Habermas's (1983a, p. 269) mistaken accusation against Rorty's position. This shows itself in Habermas's life-long scramble to grab all the extant streams of social science and commit *Aufhebung* upon them – to preserve, transcend, destroy – so that his urge to create a seamless theory – *a* theory – of social life will win acceptance as the champion over all others. Schleiermacher (or Dilthey or their modern exemplar, Emilio Betti) would find this philosophically foolish, hermeneutically impractical, and ethically repugnant.

The great gap between classic hermeneutic practice and Habermas's (1984, p. 135) scientization of it is most clear in his magnum opus, where he 'sums up' the methodological uses of philosophical hermeneutics, which amounts to a great trivialization (of Gadamer's ideas), mixed with pointless rigidification in favor of the scientism he prefers. His related fear of 'radical hermeneuticism' is fully revealed nearby.

> If *some* concept of rationality is unavoidably built into the action-theoretic foundations of sociology, then theory formation is in danger of being limited from the start to a particular, culturally or historically bound perspective, unless fundamental concepts are constructed in such a way that the concept of rationality they implicitly posit is encompassing and general, that is, satisfies universalistic claims. (Habermas, 1984, p. 137)

Compare Rorty:

> From my point of view, the attempt to develop a 'universal pragmatics' of a 'transcendental hermeneutics' is very suspicious ... I want to claim, on the contrary [after having quoted Habermas] that there is no point in trying to find a general synoptic way of 'analyzing' the 'functions knowledge has in universal contexts of practical life,' and that cultural anthropology (in a large sense which includes intellectual history) is all we need ... The objectionable self-confidence in question is simply the tendency of normal discourse to block the flow of conversation by presenting itself as offering the canonical vocabulary for discussion of a given topic – and, more importantly, the tendency of normal epistemologically centered philosophy to block the road by putting itself forward as the final commensurating vocabulary for all *possible* rational discourse. (Rorty, 1979, pp. 380, 381, 387)

It is not true that Habermas claims to be advancing the 'final commensurating vocabulary' for social theorizing, but it is likely that if his notions about rationality, hermeneutic consciousness, and universal validity claims were taken seriously, this might well be the sad result. He virtually says so himself.

> If the understanding of meaning has to be understood as communicative experience, and if this is possible only in the performative attitude of a communicative actor, the experiential basis of an interpretive sociology is compatible with its claim to objectivity only if hermeneutic procedures can be based at least intuitively on general and encompassing structures of rationality ... we cannot expect objectivity in social-theoretical knowledge if the corresponding concepts of communicative action and interpretation express a merely particular perspective on rationality, one interwoven with a particular cultural tradition ... If the requirement of objectivity is to be satisfied, this

structure would have to be shown to be *universally valid* in a specific sense. (Habermas, 1984, p. 137)

Habermas admits in his major work that he is treading ground usually reserved for philosophers, and, since Rorty says that ground recently trod by philosophers is not important anymore, he is engaging anthropolgy, sociology, and other fields in an effort to keep alive 'the conversation which Plato began'. In this odd role-trading, the sociologist comes off as 'the last great rationalist' people say he or she is, and the philosopher, who has only contempt for this or any other 'commensurating' belief-system, ends up in sociologizing knowledge via heremeneutics: 'an expression of hope that the cultural space left by the demise of epistemology [that is, thinking analogous to Habermas] will not be filled – that our culture should become one in which the demand for constraint and confrontation is no longer felt' (Rorty, 1979, p. 315). How is it that these words, which could only have gladdened Adorno, Horkheimer, or Marcuse, are proposed by the American philosopher, whereas terms taken from the arid plain of Carnap, Ayer, Hempel and other scientizers of thought once dominant in the USA fill the sociologist's book? In itself, a marvelous hermeneutic opportunity! But the real question now is from whom can the social theorist learn the most. One of the two men wrote these lines:

But the dangers to abnormal discourse do not come from science or naturalistic philosophy. They come from the scarcity of food and from the secret police. Given leisure and libraries, the conversation which Plato began will not end in self-objectivation – not because aspects of the world, or of human beings, escape being objects of scientific inquiry, but simply because free and leisured conversation generates abnormal discourse as the sparks fly upward.

The hermeneutically attuned reader will know which one. This sentiment is congenial to the collective message of Schleiermacher, Dilthey, Mead, Sullivan, even Weber on those Sunday afternoons by the Neckar when Lukács would dazzle and infuriate his guests. But it is anathema to worshippers in the temple of universal validity claims, objectivity, and general and encompassing structures of rationality known 'at least intuitively' to hold for everybody adapted to faceless domination.

Conclusion

I do not think hermeneutics can be tamed. The reason it cannot is because it is insistently axiological and practical or, in the Greek sense, it is the activity of *prudentia*, of practical rationality (cf. Gadamer, 1983, p. 127).

Gadamer's remonstrance with Schleiermacher, who himself did not escape altogether the winds of scientism, speaks just as forcefully to contemporary theorists.

> The imposition of an artificial apparatus that is supposed to open up whatever is alien and make it one's own takes the place of the communicative ability in which people live together and mediate themselves along with the tradition in which they stand. (Gadamer, 1983, p. 130)

It would indeed be a relief to find that grail of social science, the objective grounding for what in the end are a profusion of styles, demands, anxieties, cruelties, and so on; it would be nice to take the barbarism out of civilization. But the likelihood of that is like the chance of saying exactly what a text has to offer: 'The very idea of a definitive interpretation seems to be intrinsically contradictory. Interpretation is always on the way' (Gadamer, 1983, p. 105). Perhaps this explains why even a serious book like MacIntyre's *After Virtue* – a collection of interpretations 'on the way' to re-understanding a number of axiological writers – wins such a wide readership, while *The Structure of Social Action* sold 1,500 copies in its first ten years of existence. There is something beyond objective rationality, and it is living rationality, and to get to it one must practice hermeneutics, and keep practicing until you get it less wrong.

PART V

Epilog

Stephen P. Turner and Mark L. Wardell

Sociology has always had the character of a project, of a self-conscious plan to realize particular goals, goals that initially were political as well as cognitive. In contrast to the natural sciences, where 'methodology' has usually followed science by articulating the cognitive aims and standards of the most advanced fields only when their achievements were secure, discussions of the aims and failings of various conceptions of the sociological project have always been a central part of sociological discourse.[1] The goal of extending the concept of scientific law from the domains of the natural sciences to the social world was the source of what consensus existed among the major 'sociological' thinkers of the middle part of the nineteenth century – Comte, Mill, Quetelet, Spencer and (in a qualified way) Marx. But the endeavor to adopt the methodological strategy of the natural sciences has itself never been freed of the suspicion, as Harold Laski put it fifty years ago, that it is a 'great illusion' (quoted in Catlin, 1964, p. xxxi).

Around this original core were other, secondary, purposes: the critique of ideology, the institutionalization of rational politics, the edification of the masses, the solving of the problem of universal history and progress, the creation of a language of numbers representing the social realm (corresponding to the language of numbers in which Galileo had said the book of nature was written), the sanctioning of particular moral opinions and political agendas, and the quest for a new, 'scientific', standard for choosing among competing values. None of these secondary purposes was 'achieved' in any direct sense by the classical figures but, in each case, their pursuit did have practical effects. Works by sociologists increasingly have marked the practices of European and American societies and affected the policies and sensibilities of the people who made up these societies, initially the political class and later the economic elite. The claims and categories of sociologists appear in an extraordinarily diverse set of practical contexts and conversations within capitalist and socialist societies. Still, there are few serious attempts to fulfill the central theoretical aims of the classical project today – to offer an integrated view of the current political-economic world and its social life.

The projects of classical sociology, of Weber, Durkheim and Pareto, and for that matter Schutz and Parsons, were themselves successor projects, revisions both of the cognitive goals and methodological approaches of a previous generation. These revisions failed in their turn, but not without revealing a good deal in the course of their failure. As Peter Lassman shows, something of present value can be learned by analyzing Mannheim's concern for politics, something which was only *secondary* to his original, systematic purpose. The lesson may be generalized: the core of past projects, and their primary and distinctive aims and strategies, are dead, but they continue to have a 'present value' where their peripheral themes connect with present purposes.

Whatever else may be said of Foucault's historical insights, one insight has special validity – that conversations, institutional structures, forms of thought, audiences, literary styles and practices fit together. These change at rates and paces different from one another. Theoretical schemes ossify: concepts formed during one moment of change constitute institutionalized discourses of a later moment, after which they gradually lose applicability and immediacy in relation to the bodies of practice which border them, as well as the world beyond the institutional setting.

The audience and institutional setting of the transitional generation, Marx, Weber and Durkheim, were quite different from the audience and setting of the earlier generation, Spencer, Mill, Quetelet and Comte, and from those of the generations that followed. Charles Ellwood began a departmental history, written in the 1930s, with this:

> The history of the Department of Sociology of the University of Missouri has been the history of an adventure in humanitarian science. From the first the Department has been a militant organization fighting for the truth and the right. It has aroused the opposition, therefore, of those opposed to social progress on the one hand, and of those educators and scientists on the other, who claim that the scientific departments in our universities should not concern themselves with practical interests or with questions of social welfare.[2]

Ellwood's commitments to theory, research and practice were equally strong; for him they were one and the same project. Yet once the initial chairs and departments of sociology were secure and once the establishment of the welfare state made reform a matter of the internal politics of bureaucratic regimes, commitments to theory, research and reform were separated from one another. In the fervent professionalization of the discipline in the postwar years, purity became a rhetoric and the possibility of a pure sociology became an ideal. The debates about value-freedom and bias in the 1960s used this rhetoric, but they failed to transcend it. Howard Becker's Society for the Study of Social Problems Presidential Address (1967) and Alfred McClung Lee's American Sociological Association Presidential Address (1976), and more poignantly the writings of C. Wright Mill, were efforts to mediate these divisions, to make the project whole again.

Sociological theory now appears to be facing a transition in which these older lines and divisions will themselves change, for reasons that are now emerging. Contemporary political disputes over the responsibility of the state to its national community, which have been revived by recent electoral failures in welfare regimes, should have the same motivating significance for the present sociological theory that the dispute between 'the party of progress' and 'the party of order' had for Comte, or the problem of solidarity in a liberal republic had for Durkheim. They do not, and the apprehensiveness with which sociologists currently struggle to construct a new relationship with the state, as well as a 'market' of employers, an audience of materially motivated students, and hearers of other kinds who are not 'opinion leaders' but clients, program administrators and policy makers, is a sign that the core of sociological thought is presently failing in its relations with audiences that are outside the walls of disciplinary sociology.

What Alfred Ayer says of philosophers, that an 'unfortunate disparity' has developed 'between the richness of their technique and the increasing poverty of the material on which they are able to exercise it' (1977, p. 304), may be said of sociologists as well. One of the peculiar consequences of the institutionalization of intellectual life in the last half of the nineteenth century (of which the disciplinary category 'sociology' is a product) was the creation of professional discourse bounded by definitions of the subject, or by methodological traditions, which fragment the content considered relevant into the specialized 'problem' areas of the discipline. These were discontents to which Weber believed modern scholarship as a whole to be condemned. But the inevitability of specialization does not imply the permanent validity of particular divisions.

At a minimum, a realization of this sort points to the urgency of a dialogue across academic boundaries. To engage in these conversations as a co-participant requires something more than taking the stance of an analyst, as happens when sociologists engage in critiques of ideology or of the factual basis for claims in other discourses. Sociologists may need to accept some tutelage from ethics, from political theory, or even from recent literary criticism. Entering into these conversations will have fundamental implications for the present forms of the sociological tradition itself. For example, to rethink old boundaries between sociology and ethics on the basis of the present developments in ethics challenges basic assumptions of the entire sociological enterprise.

The bodies of practical discourse used by journalists, citizens, corporate managers and leaders of mass movements have also been institutionally dissociated from sociological discourse. During certain moments, such as the period of the consolidation of disciplinary sociology in the 1950s and early 1960s, the separation between practical and sociological discourses was strongly marked. Recently, in some contexts, the two have come very close to merging. The self-analysis of Solidarność (Touraine, 1983); the self-reflection of contemporary Third World Marxist movements, where the practical problems of 'development' dictate the 'theoretical' problems of applying a political rhetoric derived from nineteenth-century Europe; the discussion of the organization of work and managerial control (Braverman, 1974), such as that occasioned by computer technology and international market competition – these are examples of overlap and mutuality between practical and sociological discourse characteristic of the Webbs's social thinking during the development of the welfare state in Britain, of earlier American social science during the Progressive era, and of the sociologically orientated writings about industry by Henderson, C. I. Bernard, and Mayo during the 1930s.

The essays in this book grope along and across several borders with sociological theory on the one side, academic and practical discourses on the other. Specialization and professionalization helped to erect these borders. To be sure, the territories on the other side are unfamiliar, the paths between them and sociological theory have become overgrown. But traces of the other side have been preserved in the collective memory of the discipline; as discussed in these essays, the classical sociologists and a few of their heirs had seen the other side.[3] To cross these particular borders, to rethink the rationales on which they were laid out, and to find one's way today, inevitably calls up memories of the classics. Thus these essays have a strong historical sensibility in addition to a respect for the future.

Once lost, immediacy is difficult to regain *within* the old forms. Consequently, much that is said in this book has the purpose of placing in perspective the conceptual legacy of the recent past. Humanism, structuralism, Parsonianism, in general the image of sociology as an autonomous discipline governed by its own rules of development, present a practice as alien or subordinate to theory. To change this requires in part actively breaking down the illusion of autonomy and showing where the errors and dead ends lie, in order to free us from tacit doctrines and assumptions that, as ideologies, prevent us from participating in the larger conversations. Part of this work was intended to move toward these conversations by identifying some of the hidden obstacles to dialogue that have been woven into the institutional fabric of sociology.

The accomplishment of such a task necessarily involves criticism of the schools of sociology from a point outside of their direct theoretical influence. The essays in this book do not, therefore, represent a particular school or schools as a collection of essays in sociological theory perhaps ordinarily would, although they necessarily rely on the intellectual traditions of the entire discipline. Nor are the essays an attempt to call sociology to commitment. As we have suggested, the call to commitment, exemplified by Becker's and Lee's presidential addresses, were part of a different, older dialogue found in institutional sociology for the past sixty years. The essays are, rather, reconstructive.

The reconstruction of sociological theory must be based on something other than a renewed commitment to socialist humanism, a puristic return to the theoretical logic of 'action and order', or even a renewed attempt to mediate old antinomies among research, theory and practice. Without expanding the theoretical horizon of the present project, sociology may well be giving up the traditional task of a self-understanding of society and replacing it with a research enterprise defined by the agendas of 'clients'. Without turning to practice and to a serious participation in conversations of the ethics and politics of practice, sociology may also be giving up its traditional role as an historical agent in the emergence of society. In either case, it would be the ruin of the project intended by the classical figures. We cannot go back to their project; we can only go forward with it as our example. Perhaps the theoretical breadth of the classics and their willingness to become involved in conversations of practice were the source of their most lasting contributions to sociological theory, and their value as exemplars.

Notes

1 To be sure, the distance between articulation and achievement has varied historically; cf. Laudan, 1984. In the physics of the early twentieth century, for example, the distance was quite small; in the physics which has developed in the past half-century, the gap is quite large (Holton, 1984).

2 Quoted from Charles Ellwood, 'A history of the Department of Sociology in the University of Missouri', Bernard Papers, University of Chicago Library, Chicago.

3 Similarly, the ethics of classical philosophy (and for that matter of the Scottish moralists and the nineteenth-century utilitarians) had a sense of the socially and historically situated character of virtue and the 'good' which recent ethics and meta-ethics has lost. When MacIntyre, 1984, attempts to recapture this sense, it is by an historical narrative which is a synthesis of sociology and the intellectual history of ethical doctrines.

References

Abercrombie, N., and Urry, J. (1983), *Capital, Labour and the Middle Classes* (London: Allen & Unwin).

Alexander, J. C. (1982), *Theoretical Logic in Sociology*, Vol. I (London: Routledge & Kegan Paul).

Aron, R. (1968), *Main Currents in Sociological Thought*, Vol. II (London: Weidenfeld & Nicolson).

Aronowitz, S. (1981), *The Crisis in Historical Materialism* (New York: Praeger).

Ayer, A. J. (1977), *Part of my Life* (London: Oxford University Press).

Ball, M. *et al.* (1979), 'Marx's capital and capitalism today', *Capital and Class*, vol. 7, pp. 100–13.

Barry, B. (1970), *Sociologists, Economists and Democracy* (Chicago: University of Chicago Press).

Barry, B. and Hardin, R. (eds) (1982), *Rational Man and Irrational Society* (Beverly Hills, Calif: Sage).

Barthes, R. (1976), *The Pleasure of the Text* (London: Cape).

Becker, H. S. (1967), 'Whose side are we on?' *Social Problems*, vol. 14, pp. 239–47.

Beiner, R. (1983), *Political Judgement* (London: Methuen).

Bell, D. (1976), *The Cultural Contradictions of Capitalism* (London: Heinemann).

Bellah, R. N. (1973), 'Introduction', in R. N. Bellah (ed.), *Emile Durkheim on Morality and Society* (Chicago: University of Chicago Press), pp. ix–iv.

Bellah, R. N. (1983), 'The ethical aims of social inquiry', in N. Haan, R. N. Bellah, P. Rabinow, and W. M. Sullivan (eds), *Social Science as Moral Inquiry* (New York: Columbia University Press), pp. 360–81.

Bellah, R. N., Haan, N., Robinow, P., and Sullivan, W. M. (1983), 'Introduction', in N. Haan, R. N. Bellah, P. Rabinow, and W. M. Sullivan (eds), *Social Science as Moral Inquiry* (New York: Columbia University Press), pp. 1–18.

Berger, P., and Luckmann, T. (1967), *The Social Construction of Reality* (Garden City: Doubleday).

Berkowitz, S. D. (1981), *An Introduction to Structural Analysis* (Toronto: Butterworths).

Berlin, I. (1982 [1973]), 'The counter-Enlightenment', in H. Hardy (ed.), *Against the Current* (New York): Viking, pp. 1–24.

Blau, P. M. (1964), *Exchange and Power in Social Life* (New York: Wiley).

Blau, P. M. (1970), 'A formal theory of differentiation in organizations', *American Sociological Review*, vol. 35, no. 2, pp. 201–18.

Blau, P. M. (1974), 'Parameters of social structure', *American Sociological Review*, vol. 39, pp. 615–35.

Blau, P. M. (1977), 'A macrosociological theory of social structure', *American Journal of Sociology*, vol. 83, no. 1, pp. 26–54.

Blau, P. M. (1981), 'Diverse views of social structure and their common denominator', in P. M. Blau and R. K. Merton (eds), *Continuities in Structural Inquiry* (London: Sage), pp. 1–22.

Blumer, H. (1969), *Symbolic Interactionism* (Englewood Cliffs, NJ: Prentice-Hall).

Blumer, H. (1981), 'George Herbert Mead', in B. Rhea (ed.), *The Future of the Sociological Classics* (London: Allen & Unwin), pp. 136–69.

Bottomore, T. (1983), 'Social theory and politics in the history of social theory', in C. Lloyd (ed.), *Social Theory and Political Practice* (Oxford: Clarendon), pp. 39–60.

Bourricaud, F. (1981), *The Sociology of Talcott Parsons* (Chicago: University of Chicago Press).

Braverman, H. (1974), *Labour and Monopoly Capital* (New York: Monthly Review).

Brener, S. (1982), 'The illusion of politics: politics and rationalisation in Max Weber and George Lukács', *New German Critique*, no. 26, pp. 55–79.

Brinton, C. (1933), *English Political Thought in the Nineteenth Century* (London: Benn).

Brittan, S. (1975), 'The economic contradictions of democracy', *British Journal of Political Science*, vol. 5, pp. 129–59.

Cassirer, E. (1951 [1932]), *The Philosophy of the Enlightenment* (Princeton, NJ: Princeton University Press).

Cassirer, E. (1970 [1945]), *Rousseau, Kant, Goethe: Two Essays* (Princeton, NJ: Princeton University Press).

Catlin, G. (1964), 'Introduction to the translation', in E. Durkheim, *The Rules of Sociological Method* (New York: Free Press), pp. xi–xxxvi.

Claessens, D. (1966), 'Soziologie als Beruf und das Problem möglicher Normativität angewandter Soziologie', in D. Claessens (ed.), *Angst, Furcht und gesellschaftlicher Druck* (Dortmund: Ruhfus), pp. 9–22.

Cohen, M. (ed.) (1984), *Ronald Dworkin and Contemporary Jurisprudence* (Totowa, NJ: Rowman & Allanheld).

Comte, A. (1975 [c. 1840]), 'Social physics', in G. Lenzer (ed.), *Auguste Comte and Positivism: The Essential Writings* (New York: Harper Torchbooks), pp. 195–308.

Connolly, W. E. (1981), *Appearance and Reality in Politics* (Cambridge: Cambridge University Press).

Cousins, M., and Hussain, A. (forthcoming), *Foucault* (London: Macmillan).

Coward, R., and Ellis, J. (1977), *Language and Materialism* (London: Routledge & Kegan Paul).

Crick, B. (1980), *George Orwell: A Life* (Harmondsworth, Ind.: Penguin).

Cutler, A., Hindess, B., Hirst, P. Q., and Hussain, A. (1977), *Marx's Capital and Capitalism Today*, Vol. I (London: Routledge & Kegan Paul).

Cutler, A., Hindess, B., Hirst, P. Q., and Hussain, A. (1978), *Marx's Capital and Capitalism Today*, Vol. II (London: Routledge & Kegan Paul).

Cutler, A., Hindess, B., Hirst, P. Q., and Hussain, A. (1979), 'An imaginary orthodoxy', *Economy & Society*, vol. 8, no. 3, pp. 308–41.

Dahrendorf, R. (1968), *Essays in the Theory of Society* (London: Routledge & Kegan Paul).

Deleuze, G., and Guattari, F. (1977), *Anti-Oedipus* (New York: Viking).

Derrida, J. (1982), *Margins of Philosophy* (Chicago: University of Chicago Press).

Descombes, V. (1980), *Modern French Philosophy* (Cambridge: Cambridge University Press).

Dewey, J. (1930 [1922]), *Human Nature and Conduct: An Introduction to Social Psychology* (New York: Modern Library).

Dilthey, W. (1976), *Dilthey: Selected Writings*, trans. and ed. H. P. Rickman (Cambridge: Cambridge University Press).

Donagan, A. (1977), *Theory of Morality* (Chicago: University of Chicago Press).

Dreyfus, H. L., and Rabinow, P. (1983), *Michel Foucault: Beyond Structuralism and Hermeneutics* (Berkeley, Calif.: University of California Press).

Duncan, O. D., and Schnore, L. F. (1959), 'Cultural, behavioral and ecological perspectives in the study of social organization', *American Journal of Sociology*, vol. 65, no. 2, pp. 132–46.

Durkheim, E. (1938), *The Rules of Sociological Method*, 8th edn (Chicago: University of Chicago Press).

Durkheim, E. (1961), *Moral Education* (New York: Free Press).

Durkheim, E. (1964), *The Division of Labor in Society* (New York: Free Press).

Durkheim, E. (1966), *Suicide* (New York: Free Press).

Dworkin, R. (1977), *Taking Rights Seriously* (Cambridge, Mass.: Harvard University Press).

Eisenstadt, S. N., and Curelarau, M. (1975), *The Form of Sociology: Paradigms and Crises* (New York: Wiley).

Elias, N. (1983), *Engagement und Distanzierung*, Arbeiten zur Wissenssoziologie 1 (Frankfurt on Main: Suhrkamp).

Ellis, A., and Kumar, K. (eds) (1983), *Dilemmas of Liberal Democracies* (London: Tavistock).

Elster, J. (1978), *Logic and Society* (Chichester: Wiley).

Elster, J. (1979), *Ulysses and the Sirens* (Cambridge: Cambridge University Press).

Elster, J. (1980), 'Reply to comments', *Inquiry*, vol. 23, pp. 213–32.

Elster, J. (1982), 'Marxism, functionalism and game theory, the case for methodological individualism', *Theory & Society*, vol. 11, no. 4, pp. 453–82.

Elster, J. (1983), *Explaining Technical Change* (Cambridge: Cambridge University Press).

Faust, D. G. (ed.) (1981), *The Ideology of Slavery: Proslavery Thought in Antebellum South 1830–1860* (Baton Rouge, La: Louisiana State University Press).

Fleck, L. (1979 [1935]), *Genesis and Development of a Scientific Fact*, ed. T. D. Trenn and R. K. Merton (Chicago: University of Chicago Press).

Foucault, M. (1973), *The Birth of the Clinic* (London: Tavistock).

Foucault, M. (1977), *Discipline and Punish: The Birth of The Prison* (London: Allen Lane).

Foucault, M. (1980a), *The History of Sexuality Volume 1: An Introduction* (New York: Vintage Books).

Foucault, M. (1980b), *Power/Knowledge* (Brighton: Harvester).

Freiberg, J. W. (1979), *Critical Sociology: European Perspectives* (New York: Irvington).

Fuhrman, E. (1980), *The Sociology of Knowledge in America, 1883–1915* (Charlottesville: University Press of Virgina).

Furet, F. (1981), *Interpreting the French Revolution* (Cambridge: Cambridge University Press).

Gadamer, H.-G. (1975), *Truth & Method*, trans. G. Barden and J. Cumming (New York: Seabury).

Gadamer, H.-G. (1980), *Dialogue and Dialectic: Eight Hermeneutical Studies on Plato*, trans. P. C. Smith (New Haven, Conn.: Yale University Press).

Gadamer, H.-G. (1983), *Reason in the Age of Science*, trans. F. Lawrence (Cambridge, Mass.: MIT Press).

Gallie, W. B. (1973), 'An ambiguity in the idea of politics and its practical implications', *Political Studies*, vol. 21, no. 4, pp. 442–52.

Gay, P. (1963), *The Party of Humanity* (New York. Norton).
Gay, P. (1977), *The Enlightenment* (New York: Norton).
Gewirth, A. (1978), *Reason and Morality* (Chicago: University of Chicago Press).
Giddens, A. (1971), *Capitalism and Modern Social Theory* (Cambridge: Cambridge University Press).
Giddens, A. (1979), *Central Problems in Social Theory* (London: Macmillan).
Gieryn, T. (1983), 'Boundary-work and the demarcation of science from non-science: strains and interests in professional ideologies of scientists', *American Sociological Review*, vol. 48, pp. 781-95.
Goffman, E. (1959), *The Presentation of Self in Everyday Life* (Garden City, NY: Doubleday).
Goffman, E. (1967), *Interaction Ritual: Essays in Face-to-Face Behavior* (Chicago: Aldine).
Goffman, E. (1971), *Relations in Public: Microstudies of the Public Order* (New York: Basic Books).
Goffman, E. (1981). *Forms of Talk* (Philadelphia, Pa: University of Pennsylvania Press).
Gouldner, A. W. (1965), *Enter Plato* (New York: Basic Books).
Gouldner, A. W. (1970), *The Coming Crisis of Western Sociology* (New York: Basic Books).
Gouldner, A. W. (1973), *For Sociology: Renewal and Critique in Sociological Theory*, ed. A. W. Gouldner (Harmondsworth, Ind.: Penguin).
Granovetter, M. S. (1973), 'The strength of weak ties', *American Journal of Sociology*, vol. 78, no. 6, pp. 1360-80.
Habermas, J. (1970), *Toward a Rational Society* (Boston, Mass.: Beacon).
Habermas, J. (1971), *Knowledge and Human Interests* (Boston, Mass.: Beacon).
Habermas, J. (1974 [1963]), *Theory and Practice* (London: Heinemann).
Habermas, J. (1983a), 'Interpretive social science vs. hermeneuticism', in N. Haan, R. N. Bellah, P. Rabinow, and W. M. Sullivan (eds), *Social Science as Moral Inquiry* (New York: Columbia University Press), pp. 251-69.
Habermas, J. (1983b), *Philosophical-Political Profiles*, trans. F. G. Lawrence (Cambridge, Mass.: MIT Press).
Habermas, J. (1984), *The Theory of Communicative Action, Vol. 1: Reason and the Rationalization of Society*, trans. T. McCarthy (Boston, Mass.: Beacon).
Hampshire, S. (1973), 'Political theory and theory of knowledge', *Twentieth Century Studies*, no. 9, pp. 70-5.
Hanneman, R. (1983), 'Review of Hauser, et al., *Social Structure and Behavior*', *Contemporary Sociology*, vol. 12, no. 6, pp. 639-40.
Hanson, N. R. (1965), *Patterns of Discovery* (Cambridge: Cambridge University Press).
Hardin, R. (1982), *Collective Action* (Baltimore, Md: Johns Hopkins University Press).
Harris, L. (1978), 'The science of the economy', *Economy & Society*, vol. 7, no. 3, pp. 284-320.
Heath, A. (1976), *Rational Choice and Social Exchange* (Cambridge: Cambridge University Press).
Hindess, B. (1977), 'Humanism and teleology in sociological theory', in B. Hindess (ed.), *Sociological Theories of the Economy* (London: Macmillan), pp. 157-89.

Hindess, B. (1983), *Parliamentary Democracy and Socialist Politics* (London: Routledge & Kegan Paul).

Hindess, B. (1984), 'Rational choice theory and the analysis of political action', *Economy & Society*, vol. 13, no. 3, pp. 255–77.

Hindess, B., and Hirst, P. (1975), *Pre-Capitalist Modes of Production* (London: Routledge & Kegan Paul).

Hindess, B., and Hirst, P. (1977), *Mode of Production and Social Formation* (London: Macmillan).

Hirsch, F. (1977), *Social Limits to Growth* (London: Routledge & Kegan Paul).

Hirschman, A. O. (1971), *A Bias for Hope: Essays on Development and Latin America* (New Haven, Conn.: Yale University Press).

Hirschman, A. O. (1983), 'Morality and the social sciences', in N. Haan, R. N. Bellah, P. Rabinow, and W. M. Sullivan (eds), *Social Science as Moral Inquiry* (New York: Columbia University Press), pp. 21–32.

Hirst, P. (1979), *On Law & Ideology* (London: Macmillan).

Hirst, P., and Woolley, P. (1982), *Social Relations & Human Attributes* (London: Tavistock).

Hobbes, T. (1969 [1651]), *Leviathan* (New York: Washington Square).

Hollis, M., and Lukes, S. (eds) (1982), *Rationality and Relativism* (Oxford: Blackwell).

Holton, G. (1984), 'Do scientists need a philosophy?', *The Times Literary Supplement*, 2 November, pp. 1231–4.

Homans, G. (1961), *Social Behavior: Its Elementary Forms* (New York: Harcourt Brace Jovanovich).

Hopkins, C. H. (1940), *The Rise of the Social Gospel in American Protestantism, 1865–1915* (New Haven, Connecticut: Yale University Press).

Horowitz, I. L. (1974), 'Capitalism, communism, and multinationalism', in I. L. Horowitz (ed.), *Ideology and Utopia in the United States, 1956–1976* (New York: Oxford University Press).

Hughes, H. (1968 [1854]), *A Treatise on Sociology* (New York: Negro Universities Press).

Illich, I. (1978), *Limits to Medicine, Medical Nemesis: The Expropriation of Health* (London: Pelican).

Jaeger, W. (1945), *Paedeia: The Ideals of Greek Culture*, Vol. 1, 2nd edn, trans. G. Highet (New York: Oxford University Press).

James, W. (1907), *Pragmatism: A New Name for Some Old Ways of Thinking* (New York: Longmans, Green).

Kant, I. (1956), *Foundations of the Metaphysics of Morals* (Indianapolis, Ind.: Bobbs-Merrill).

Kerblay, B. (1983), *Modern Soviet Society* (New York: Pantheon).

Koyre, A. (1968), *Metaphysics and Measurement* (London: Chapman & Hall).

Kuhn, T. (1962), *The Structure of Scientific Revolutions* (Chicago: University of Chicago Press).

Lacan, J. (1984), *Les Complexes familiaux dans la formation de l'individu* (Paris: Navarin/Seuil).

Lakatos, I., and Musgrave, A. (eds) (1970), *Criticism and the Growth of Knowledge* (Cambridge: Cambridge University Press).

Lane, M. (1970), *Introduction to Structuralism* (New York: Basic Books).

Lasch, C. (1983), *The Culture of Narcissism* (New York: Warner Books).

Lash, S. (1984a), 'Genealogy and the body: Foucault/Deleuze/Nietzsche', *Theory, Culture & Society*, vol. 2, no. 2, pp. 1–18.

Lash, S. (1984b), *The Militant Worker: Class and Radicalism in France and America* (London: Heinemann).

Lash, S., and Urry, J. (1984), 'The new Marxism of collective action: a critical analysis', *Sociology*, vol. 18, pp. 33–50.

Lash, S., and Urry, J. (1985), *Space, Class and Culture: Disorganised Capitalism in Comparative Perspective* (Cambridge: Polity).

Lassman, P. (1982), 'Raiders of the lost paradigm', *Sociology*, vol. 16, pp. 290–98.

Laudan, L. (1984), *Science and Values: The Aims of Science and Their Role in Scientific Debate* (Berkeley, Calif.: University of California Press).

Lee, A. M. (1976), 'Presidential address: sociology for whom?', *American Sociological Review*, vol. 41, pp. 925–36.

Levi, I. (1982), 'Conflict and social agency', *The Journal of Philosophy*, vol. 79, no. 5, pp. 231–47.

Lipset, S. M. (1979), *The First New Nation: The United States in Historical and Comparative Perspective*, revised edn (New York: Norton).

Lipset, S. M., and Smelser, N. J. (1961), 'The setting of sociology in the 1950's', in S. M. Lipset and N. J. Smelser (eds), *Sociology* (Englewood Cliffs, NJ: Prentice-Hall), pp. 1–13.

Louch, A. R. (1966), *Explanation and Human Action* (Oxford: Blackwell).

Lukács, G. (1980), *The Destruction of Reason*, trans., P. Palmer (London: Merlin).

Lyman, S. M. (1975), 'Legitimacy and consensus in Lipset's America: from Washington to Watergate', *Social Research*, vol. 42, pp. 729–59.

Lyman, S. M. (1984), 'Interactionism and race relations at the macrosocietal level: the contribution of Herbert Blumer', *Symbolic Interaction*, vol. 7, pp. 107–20.

Lyotard, J. F. (1973), *Dérive à partir de Marx et Freud* (Paris: UGE).

Lyotard, J. F. (1980a), 'Freud selon Cezanne', in J. F. Lyotard (ed.) *Des Dispositifs pulsionnels* (Paris: Christian Bourgois), pp. 67–88.

Lyotard, J. F. (1980b), 'Sur une figure de discours', in J. F. Lyotard (ed.), *Des Dispositifs pulsionnels* (Paris: Christian Bourgois), pp. 127–47.

McDermott, J. G. (1969), 'The American context', in J. G. McDermott (ed.), *Basic Writings of Josiah Royce*, Vol. I (Chicago: University of Chicago Press).

MacIntyre, A. (1972), 'Is a science of comparative politics possible?', in P. Laslett *et al.* (eds), *Philosophy, Politics and Society*, 4th series (Oxford: Blackwell).

MacIntyre, A. (1980 [1967]), *A Short History of Ethics* (London: Routledge & Kegan Paul).

MacIntyre, A. (1981), *After Virtue: A Study in Moral Theory* (Paris: University of Notre Dame Press).

MacPherson, C. B. (1972), *The Political Theory of Possessive Individualism* (New York: Oxford University Press).

Mannheim, K. (1936), *Ideology and Utopia* (London: Routlege & Kegan Paul).

Mannheim, K. (1940), *Man and Society in an Age of Reconstruction: Studies in Modern Social Structure* (London: Routledge & Kegan Paul).

Mannheim, K. (1943), *Diagnosis of Our Time: Wartime Essays by a Sociologist* (London: Routledge & Kegan Paul).

Mannheim, K. (1971 [1927]), 'Conservative thought', in K. H. Wolff (ed.), *From Karl Mannheim* (New York: Oxford University Press), pp. 132–222.

Marx, K. (1964), *Karl Marx: Early Writings*, trans. and ed. T. B. Bottomore (New York: McGraw-Hill).

Marx, K. (1965a), *The 18th Brumaire of Louis Bonaparte* (New York: International Publishers).

Marx, K. (1965b), *Karl Marx: Selected Writings in Sociology and Social Philosophy*, trans. T. B. Bottomore (New York: McGraw-Hill).

Marx, K. (1967), *The German Ideology* (New York: International Publishers).

Marx, K. (1976), *Capital*, Vol. 1, trans. B. Fowks (New York: Vintage Books).

Marx, K. (1977 [1859]), 'Preface to a critique of political economy', in D. McLellan (ed.), *Karl Marx: Selected Writings* (Oxford: Oxford University Press).

Mayer, J. P. (1956), *Max Weber and German Politics*, 2nd edn (London: Faber & Faber).

Mayhew, B. H. (1980), 'Structuralism versus individualism: Parts I and II', *Social Forces*, vol. 59, nos. 2 and 3, pp. 335–75, 627–48.

Mead, G. H. (1964a), 'The genesis of the self and social control', in A. J. Reck (ed.) *Selected Writings* (Indianapolis, Ind.: Bobbs-Merrill), pp. 267–93.

Mead, G. H. (1964b), 'The philosophies of Royce, James, and Dewey in their American setting', in A. J. Reck (ed.), *Selected Writings* (Indianapolis, Ind.: Bobbs-Merrill), pp. 371–91.

Merton, R. K. (1938), 'Social structure and anomie', *American Sociological Review*, vol. 3, no. 5, pp. 672–82.

Merton, R. K. (1957), *Social Theory and Social Structure*, enlarged edn (Glencoe, Ill.: Free Press).

Merton, R. K. (1967), *On Theoretical Sociology* (New York: Free Press).

Merton, R. K. (1975), 'Structural analysis in sociology', in P. M. Blau (ed.), *Approaches to the Study of Social Structure* (New York: Free Press), pp. 21–52.

Mills, C. W. (1961), *The Sociological Imagination* (New York: Grove).

Minson, J. (1980), 'Strategies for socialists? Foucault's conception of power', *Economy & Society*, vol. 9, no. 1, pp. 1–44.

Mitchell, J. (1982), 'Introduction I', in J. Mitchell and J. Rose (eds), *Feminine Sexuality* (London: Macmillan), pp. 1–26.

Moore, B., Jr (1973), *Reflections on the Causes of Human Misery* (Boston, Mass.: Beacon).

Moore, B., Jr (1978), *Injustice: The Social Bases of Obedience and Revolt* (White Plains, NY: M. E. Sharpe).

Morgan, E. S. (ed.) (1965), *Puritan Political Ideas, 1558–1794* (Indianapolis, Ind.: Bobbs-Merrill).

Navarro, V. (1979), 'Social class, political power, and the state: their implications in medicine', in J. D. Freiberg (ed.), *Critical Sociology: European Perspectives* (New York: Irvington), pp. 297–344.

Niebuhr, R. (1964), *Schleiermacher on Christ and Religion* (New York: Charles Scribner's Sons).

Nietzsche, F. (1967), *The Will to Power*, trans. W. Kaufmann and R. J. Hollingdale (New York: Random House).

Nisbet, R. (1968), *Tradition and Revolt* (New York: Vintage Books).

Nozick, R. (1974), *Anarchy, State and Authority* (New York: Basic Books).

Offe, C. (1985), *Disorganized Capitalism: The Transformation of Work and Politics* (Cambridge: Polity).

Offe, C., and Wiesenthal, H. (1980), 'Two logics of collective action: theoretical notes on social class and organizational form', *Political Power and Social Theory*, vol. 1, pp. 67–115.

Olson, M. (1965), *The Logic of Collective Action* (Cambridge, Mass.: Harvard University Press).

O'Neill, J. (1972), *Sociology as a Skin Trade: Essays Towards a Reflexive Sociology* (New York: Harper & Row).

O'Neill, J. (1976), 'The Hobbesian problem in Marx and Parsons', in J. J. Loubser, R. C. Baum, A. Effrat, and V. M. Lidz (eds), *Explorations in General Theory in Social Science: Essays in Honor of Talcott Parsons* (New York: Free Press), pp. 295–308.

O'Neill, J. (1979), 'The mutuality of accounts: an essay on trust', in S. G. McNall (ed.), *Theoretical Perspectives in Sociology* (New York: St. Martin's), pp. 369–80.

O'Neill, J. (1983a), 'Mutual knowledge', in D. R. Sabia, Jr, and G. Wallulis (eds), *Changing Social Science: Critical Theory and Other Critical Perspectives* (Albany, NY: State University of New York Press), pp. 53–70.

O'Neill, J. (1983b), 'Reflection and radical finitude', *Journal of the British Society for Phenomenology*, vol. 14, no. 1, pp. 17–22.

O'Neill, J. (1983c), 'Some issues in the real use of science', in B. Holzner, K. Knorr, and H. Strasser (eds), *Realizing Social Science Knowledge* (Vienna: Physica-Verlag), pp. 64–70.

O'Neill, J. (1985), *Five Bodies: Studies in Radical Anthropomorphism* (Ithaca, NY: Cornell University Press).

Parsons, T. (1936a), 'On certain sociological elements in Professor Taussig's thought', in *Explorations in Economics: Notes and Essays Contributed in Honor of F. W. Taussig* (New York: McGraw-Hill), pp. 352–79.

Parsons, T. (1936b), 'Review of Alexander von Schelting's Max Webers Wissenschaftslehre', *American Sociological Review*, vol. 1, no. 4, pp. 675–81.

Parsons, T. (1937), *The Structure of Social Action* (New York: Free Press).

Parsons, T. (1940), 'The motivation of economic activities', *Canadian Journal of Economics and Political Science*, vol. 6, pp. 187–203. Reprinted in N. Smelser (ed.) (1965), *Readings in Economic Sociology* (Englewood Cliffs, NJ: Prentice Hall), pp. 53–66.

Parsons, T. (1951), *The Social System* (New York: Free Press).

Parsons, T. (1954 [1945]) 'The present position and prospects of systematic theory in sociology', *Essays in Sociological Theory* (New York: Free Press), pp. 212–37.

Parsons, T. (1961), 'Some problems confronting sociology as a profession', in S. M. Lipset and N. J. Smelser (eds), *Sociology* (Englewood Cliffs, NJ: Prentice-Hall), pp. 14–30.

Parsons, T. (1964), 'Levels of organization and the mediation of social interaction', *Sociological Inquiry*, vol. 34, no. 2, pp. 207–20.

Parsons, T. (1965), *Social Structure and Personality* (New York: Free Press).

Parsons, T. (1967), *Sociological Theory and Modern Society* (New York: Free Press).

Parsons, T. (1968), 'An overview', in T. Parsons (ed.), *American Sociology* (New York: Basic Books), pp. 319–35.

Parsons, T. (1971), 'Value freedom and objectivity', in O. Stammer (ed.), *Max Weber and Sociology Today* (Oxford: Blackwell).

Parsons, T. (1978), *Action Theory and the Human Condition* (New York: Free Press).

Parsons, T. (1979), 'The symbolic environment of modern economies', *Social Research*, vol. 46, pp. 436–53.

Poggi, G. (1972), *Image of Society* (London: Oxford University Press).

Polanyi, K. (1944), *The Great Transformation* (Boston, Mass.: Beacon).

Polanyi, M. (1964), *Personal Knowledge* (New York: Harper & Row).

Rawls, J. (1971), *A Theory of Justice* (Cambridge, Mass.: Harvard University Press).

Renner, K. (1949), *The Institutions of Private Law and Their Social Function* (London: Routledge & Kegan Paul).

Rhea, B. (ed.) (1981), *The Future of the Sociological Classics* (London: Allen & Unwin).

Rieff, P. (1966), *The Triumph of the Therapeutic: Uses of Faith after Freud* (London: Chatto & Windus).

Roemer, J. (1981), *Analytical Foundations of Marxian Economic Theory* (Cambridge: Cambridge University Press).

Roemer, J. (1982a), 'Methodological individualism and deductive Marxism', *Theory & Society*, vol. 11, no. 4, pp. 253–87.

Roemer, J. (1982b), 'New directions in the Marxian theory of exploitation and class', *Politics & Society*, vol. 11, no. 3, pp. 375–94.

Rorty, R. (1979), *Philosophy and the Mirror of Nature* (Princeton, NJ: Princeton University Press).

Rorty, R. (1982), *Consequences of Pragmatism* (Minneapolis, Minn.: University of Minnesota Press).

Rorty, R. (1983), 'Method and morality', in N. Haan, R. N. Bellah, P. Rabinow, and W. M. Sullivan (eds) *Social Science as Moral Inquiry* (New York: Columbia University Press), pp. 155–76.

Ross, E. A. (1914 [1901]), *Social Control* (New York: Macmillan).

Rousseau, J.-J. (1947 [1791]), *The Social Contract* (New York: Hafner).

Royce, J. (1908a), 'The Pacific Coast: a psychological study of the relations of climate and civilization', *Race Questions, Provincialism, and Other American Problems* (New York: Macmillan), pp. 167–225.

Royce, J. (1908b), 'Race questions and prejudices', *Race Questions, Provincialism, and Other American Problems* (New York: Macmillan), pp. 1–54.

Royce, J. (1916), *The Philosophy of Loyalty* (New York: Macmillan).

Royce, J. (1948), *California: From the Conquest in 1846 to the Second Vigilance Committee in San Francisco* (New York: Knopf).

Royce, J. (1968 [1918]), *The Problem of Christianity* (Chicago: University of Chicago Press).

Royce, J. (1969), *The Basic Writings of Josiah Royce*, Vols I and II, ed. J. G. McDermott (Chicago: University of Chicago Press).

Safonan, M. (1968), 'De la structure en psychanalyse, contribution à une théorie du manque', in F. Wahl (ed.), *Qu'est-ce que le structuralisme?* (Paris: Seuil).

Savage, S. (1981), *The Theories of Talcott Parsons* (London: Macmillan.

Schleiermacher, F. E. D. (1973 [1836]), *Introductions to the Dialogues of Plato*, trans. W. Dobson (New York: Arno).

Schleiermacher, F. E. D. (1977), *Hermeneutics: The Handwritten Manuscripts*, ed. H. Kimmerle, trans. J. Duke and J. Forstman (Missoula, MT: Scholars Press).

Schnore, L. F. (1958), 'Social morphology and human ecology', *American Journal of Sociology*, vol. 63, no. 6, pp. 620–34.

Schwendinger, H., and Schwendinger, J., (1974), *The Sociologists of the Chair* (New York: Basic Books).

Shils, E. (1981), *Tradition* (Chicago: University of Chicago Press).

Sica, A. (1981), 'Hermeneutics and social theory', *Current Perspectives in Social Theory: A Research Annual*, vol. 2, pp. 39–54.

Simmel, G. (1965), *Essays on Sociology, Philosophy and Aesthetics*, ed. K. Wolff (New York: Harper & Row).

Sjoberg, G., Vaughan, T. R., and Sjoberg, A. F. (1984), 'Morals and behavioral research', *Journal of Applied Behavioral Science*, vol. 20, no. 4, pp. 311–22.

Smelser, N. J. (1969), 'The optimum scope of sociology', in R. Bierstedt (ed.), *A Design for Sociology: Scope, Objectives and Methods* (Philadelphia, Pa.: The American Academy of Political and Social Science), pp. 1–21.

Smith, A. (1967 [1776]), *The Wealth of Nations* (New York: Modern Library).

Sorokin, P. (1947), *Society, Culture and Personality* (New York: Harper & Brothers Publishers).

Stark, W. (1958), *The Sociology of Knowledge* (London: Routledge & Kegan Paul).

Starr, P. (1982), *The Social Transformation of American Medicine* (New York: Basic Books).

Stehr, N. (1979), 'The diversity of modes of discourse and the development of sociological knowledge', *Zeitschrift für allgemeine Wissenschaftstheorie*, vol. 10, pp. 141–61.

Stehr, N., and Meja, V. (1982), 'Zur gegenwärtigen Lage wissenssoziologischer Konzeptionen' in V. Meja and N. Stehr (eds), *Der Streit um die Wissenssoziologie, Vol. 2: Rezeption und Kritik des Wissenssoziologie* (Frankfurt on Main: Suhrkamp), pp. 893–946.

Stehr, N., and Meja, V. (1985), 'Robert K. Mertons strukturelle analyse' in K.-S. Rehberg (ed.), *Gesellschaftstheorien*, 2 vols. (Frankfurt on Main: Suhrkamp).

Stinchcombe, A. (1975), 'Merton's theory of social structure' in L. A. Coser (ed.), *The Idea of Social Structure* (New York: Harcourt Brace Jovanovich), pp. 11–34.

Stinchcombe, A. (1980), 'Is the prisoners' dilemma all of sociology?', *Inquiry*, vol. 23, pp. 187–92.

Sumner, W. G. (1940 [1906]), *Folkways* (New York: Ginn).

Sumner, W. G., and Keller, A. G. (1927), *The Science of Society*, 4 vols., (New Haven, Conn.: Yale University Press).

Suppe, F. (1977), *The Structure of Scientific Theories*, 2nd edn (Urbana, Ill.: University of Illinois Press).

Takaki, R. T. (1971), *A Pro-Slavery Crusade: The Agitation to Reopen The African Slave Trade* (New York: Free Press).

Taussig, F. W. (1906), 'The love of wealth and public service', *Publications of the American Economic Association*, 3rd series, vol. VII, pp. 1–3.

Taylor, C. (1971), 'Interpretation and the sciences of man', *Review of Metaphysics*, vol. 25, no. 1, pp. 3–51.

Taylor, C. (1980), 'Formal theory in social science', *Inquiry*, vol. 23, pp. 139–44.

Taylor, M. (1982), *Community, Anarchy and Liberty* (London: Cambridge University Press).

Tejera, V. (1979), 'Cultural analysis and interpretation in the human sciences', *Man and World*, vol. 12, pp. 192–204.

Toulmin, S. (1976a), 'How we can reconnect the sciences with the foundations of ethics', in D. Callahan and H. T. Englehardt Jr (eds), *The Roots of Ethics: Science, Religion and Values* (New York: Plenum), pp. 403–23.

Toulmin, S. (1976b), 'The moral psychology of science', in D. Callahan and H. T. Engelhardt Jr (eds), *The Roots of Ethics: Science, Religion and Values* (New York: Plenum), pp. 223–42.

Touraine, A., Dubet, F., Wiéviocka, M., and Strzelecki, J. (1983), *Solidarity; The Analysis of a Social Movement: Poland 1980–1981* (Cambridge: Cambridge University Press).

Turner, J. H. (1979), 'Sociology as a theory building enterprise', *Pacific Sociological Review*, vol. 22, no. 4, pp. 427–56.

Turner, S. P. (1977), 'Blau's theory of differentiation: Is it explanatory?', *The Sociological Quarterly*, vol. 18, pp. 17–32.

Unger, R. M. (1976), *Law in Modern Society: Toward a Criticism of Social Theory* (New York: Free Press).

Urry, J. (1981), *The Anatomy of Capitalist Societies* (London: Macmillian).

Vaughan, T., and Sjoberg, G. (1984), 'The individual and bureaucracy: an alternative Meadian interpretation', *Journal of Applied Behavioral Science*, vol. 20, no. 1, pp. 57–69.

Vidich, A. J., and Lyman, S. M. (1985), *American Sociology: Worldly Rejections of Religion and Their Directions* (New Haven, Conn.: Yale University Press).

von Schelting, A. (1934), *Max Webers Wissenschaftslehre* (Tübingen: J. C. B. Mohr [Paul Siebeck]).

Wallerstein, I. (1983), *Historical Capitalism* (London: Verso).

Wardell, M. L., and Fuhrman, E. R. (1981), 'Controversy and ideological hegemony in sociological theory', *The Sociological Quarterly*, vol. 22, no. 4, pp. 479–93.

Warriner, C. (1981), 'Levels in the study of social structure'; in P. M. Blau and R. K. Merton (eds), *Continuities in Structural Inquiry* (London: Sage), pp. 179–90.

Weber, M. (1946), *From Max Weber: Essays in Sociology*, eds H. H. Gerth and C. W. Mills (London: Routledge & Kegan Paul).

Weber, M. (1949), *The Methodology of the Social Sciences* (New York: Free Press).

Weber, M. (1951 [1922]), *Gesammelte Aufsätze zur Wissenschaftslehre* (Tübingen: J. C. B. Mohr [Paul Siebeck]).

Weber, M. (1963), *The Sociology of Religion*, trans., E. Fischoff (Boston, Mass.: Beacon).

Weber, M. (1964), *The Theory of Social and Economic Organization* (New York: Free Press).

Weber, M. (1978), *Economy and Society*, Vol. II, eds G. Roth and C. Wittich (Berkeley, Calif.: University of California Press).

Westermarck, E. (1970 [1932]), *Ethical Relativity* (Westport, Conn.: Greenwood).

White, H. C., Boorman, S. A. and Breiger, R. L. (1976), 'Social structure from multiple networks: parts I and II', *American Journal of Sociology*, vol. 81, nos. 4 and 6, pp. 730–81, 1384–446.

Whitehead, A. N. (1958 [1929]), *The Function of Reason* (Boston, Mass.: Beacon).

Wickham, G. (1983), 'Power and power analysis: beyond Foucault', *Economy & Society*, vol. 12, no. 4, pp. 468–98.

Wiley, N. (1979), 'The rise and fall of dominating theories in American sociology', in W. E. Snizek, E. R. Fuhrman, and M. Miller (eds), *Contemporary Issues in Theory and Research* (Westport, Conn.: Greenwood), pp. 47–79.

Wilson, H. T. (1977), *The American Ideology: Science, Technology and Organization as Modes of Rationality in Advanced Industrial Societies* (London: Routledge & Kegan Paul).

Winch, P. (1958), *The Idea of a Social Science* (London: Routledge & Kegan Paul).

Winter, S. G. (1964), 'Economic natural selection and the theory of the firm', *Yale Economic Essays*, vol. 4, no. 1, pp. 225–72.

Winter, S. G. (1971), 'Satisficing, selection and the innovating remnant', *Quarterly Journal of Economics*, vol. 85, no. 2, pp. 237–61.

Winter, S. G. (1975), 'Optimization and evolution', in R. H. Day and T. Groves (eds), *Adaptive Economic Models* (New York: Academic Press), pp. 73–118.

Wolin, S. (1960), *Politics and Vision* (Boston, Mass.: Little Brown).

Wolin, S. (1974), 'Gilding the iron cage', *New York Review of Books*, 24 January, pp. 40–2.

Wolin, S. (1980), 'Political theory and political commentary', in M. Richter (ed.), *Political Theory and Political Education* (Princeton, NJ: Princeton University Press), pp. 190–203.

Wolin, S. (1981), 'Max Weber: legitimation, method and theory', *Political Theory*, vol. 9, no. 3, pp. 401–24.

Wrong, D. (1961), 'The oversocialized conception of man in modern sociology', *American Sociological Review*, vol. 26, no. 2, pp. 183–93.

Index